D1026586

WEBER'S GUIDE TO PIPES AND PIPE SMOKING

Carl Weber

WEBER'S GUIDE
TO PIPES &
PIPE SMOKING

CARL WEBER

Illustrated by Charles Fellows

CORNERSTONE LIBRARY NEW YORK

CORNERSTONE LIBRARY PUBLICATIONS ARE DISTRIBUTED BY
AFFILIATED PUBLISHERS, A DIVISION OF POCKET BOOKS, INC.
ROCKEFELLER CENTER, 630 FIFTH AVENUE, NEW YORK 20, N.Y.

MANUFACTURED IN THE UNITED STATES OF AMERICA

CONTENTS

Foreword

No one really knows why men smoke. Yet long before the dis-
covery of tobacco, smoking had become the abiding joy of many
peoples. Since tobacco's discovery, smoking has truly become
one of mankind's most pleasurable pastimes.

The modern smoker has three means of enjoying this universal
practice: through cigarettes, cigars, and the pipe. And of these
three, the pipe gives the smoker lasting pleasure and the greatest
solace.

We are all aware that the pipe smoker belongs to a breed apart
from other men. His pleasures are contemplation and relaxation;
he does not rush, he is not nervous. His joys are the casual and
meditative ones, those of the fireside, the easy chair, and the good
book. The pipe stands as a symbol of this type of man, easily
recognized by his even frame of mind, his unhurried approach
to life's problems. It is almost always just such a man who chooses
a pipe as his path to smoking enjoyment.

What gives a pipe this special position in the smoker's world?
For one thing, a pipe is more than an instrument for smoking. It
is also an object of beauty, usually made of finely finished rare
briar. A pipe is agreeable to handle, to look at, and to hold. It
elicits the respect that a finely crafted product deserves.

Moreover, a pipe must be filled, lighted, and smoked with
reasonable care. The cigarette smoker, who hurriedly picks up

a pipe at an odd moment, will fill it sloppily, light it unevenly, and smoke it too rapidly. The real pipe-smoker soon learns that pipe smoking is both an art and a science. The pipe responds to its owner with exactly the same treatment that it receives from him. The man who masters the techniques of pipe smokng is re-paid by a satisfying smoke, a joy which he created for himself with his own hands.

The road to true pipe smoking pleasure is neither long nor hard. A good pipe properly filled with carefully selected tobac-cos, and smoked with care and skill, will reward its owner with unmatched taste and aroma. The pipe smoker never seeks stim-ulation through inhaling. On the contrary, the very act of lighting the pipe and smoking it will take his mind off his troubles and induce a relaxed frame of mind.

The sole purpose of this book is to help the smoker achieve these rare moments of serenity, which are increasingly hard to come by in the accelerating pace of the modern world.

CARL WEBER,
Founder, Weber Briars, Inc.

WEBER'S GUIDE TO PIPES AND PIPE SMOKING

Carl Weber

Chapter 1

What is a Pipe?

A PIPE IS NOTHING MORE than a bowl to hold burning tobacco, and a tube through which the smoke may be drawn into the mouth. But this seemingly simple device is the result of a surprising amount of skill, industry, and science. In a thousand years of smoking, the Indians of North and South America evolved only crude, clumsy pipes fashioned of coarse pottery or stone. The modern pipe, on the other hand, is the creation of European craftsmen, who brought their art to perfection over a period of more than four centuries.

The five basic parts of today's pipe are: (1) the *bowl,* in which the tobacco is burned; (2) the *shank,* usually a part of the bowl; (3) the *stem,* (commonly made of vulcanite, a form of hard rubber) which fits tightly into the shank; (4) the *lip,* a slight flange on the mouthpiece end of the stem; and (5) the *filter,* generally of metal, and attached to the stem.

When the pipe is assembled, the smoke travels from the bottom of the bowl, through the shank, around the filter, through the stem, and into the mouth. The lip prevents the stem from slipping between the smoker's teeth. Each one of these parts helps determine the quality of the smoke entering the smoker's mouth. Their design displays the end result of years of trial and error, of luck and experiment.

Fashioning a pipe by hand is a delicate operation. The briar or other pipe material must be carefully chosen, the bowl must be carved and hollowed out, the stem bored and fitted. Many ancient or primitive peoples found that making a pipe called for a great deal of effort, and they valued their pipes accordingly.

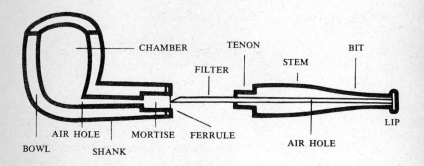

THE PARTS OF THE PIPE

Makeshift pipes were contrived from whatever substances happened to be available. In the Orient, the Chinese created pipes from hollow bamboo; the Indians of Nova Scotia made pipes from hollowed-out lobster claws, drawing the smoke through a hole pierced in a claw's narrow end. In Asia and Africa, "earth smoking" was a common practice. According to this technique, a pit dug into the soil served as the "pipe" bowl, and a hollow reed driven into the bottom of the pit as the "stem."

Primitive pipes were widely used by the Mayas of Central America more than 1,000 years ago. The Mayas also had tobacco, a plant native only to the Americas. Stone carvings found on Mayan ruins actually portray priests blowing smoke as part of a religious ritual. Their pipe was no more than a straight, tapering tube, with the tobacco at its wide end and its narrow end lodged in the priest's mouth.

The Mayas probably passed on their smoking habits to the Aztecs of Mexico, who had tubular pipes made of silver, wood, bone, reed, pottery and tortoise shell. The straight tube pipe had a major disadvantage, however, in that the tobacco could easily fall out of the tube if the smoker failed to hold his head up. Eventually, pipe-makers began bending the tobacco-holding end of the tube upward, until the pipe evolved into a bowl with an attached stem.

Pipes with small bowls were popular among the early European sailors returning from colonial America. The North American Indians smoked one such pipe, the famous calumet, or "peace pipe," consisting of a long stem made of ashwood and a "pipestone" bowl. The Indians decorated the calumet pipe with carvings, horsehair, and bird feathers. To the Indians, the mysteries of tobacco smoke and fire reflected the supernatural powers of the sun, which they worshipped.

Nicotiana tabacum and *Nicotiana rustica,* the two plants from which we obtain our modern tobacco leaves, were present in both North and South America centuries before the discovery of the New World. The plants grew sparsely, however, and their rare leaves were regarded by the Indians of North America as a gift from the gods.

These Indians often economized their tobacco by blending it with sumac leaves, the bark of the dogwood tree, the inner bark of the willow, and the leaves and bark of several other shrubs. Years ago, pure tobacco, taken so much for granted today, was a luxury not only to the Indians, but to Europeans as well. In Britain, henbane or moss was often used to adulterate the tobacco; in far-off Tibet, wild rhubarb root was mixed with it.

But the practice of smoking was never limited by the availability of tobacco. Hundreds of years before America and the tobacco plant were known to exist, people in many other parts of the world gained pleasure from smoking various kinds of herbs. The Congo pygmies, for example, were accustomed to smoking a concoction of charcoal and smoldering leaves, using a three-foot length of bamboo cane as a pipe.

Smoking may have been practiced more than 2,000 years ago, according to the ancient Greek historian, Herodotus. He describes Scythian tribesmen in Asia Minor, who "have a tree which bears the strangest produce. When they are met together in companies, they throw some of it upon the fire 'round which they are sitting, and presently, by the mere smell of the fumes which it gives out in burning, they grow drunk, as the Greeks do with wine. More of the fruit is then thrown on the fire, and their drunkenness increasing, they often jump up and begin to dance and sing. Such is the

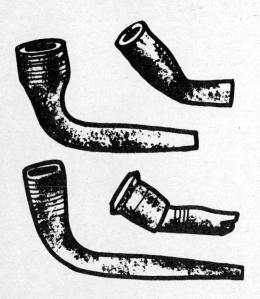

These four early American pipes, formed from pottery, are believed to have been smoked before Columbus discovered America. The two smaller ones were found in Georgia, the larger ones in New York state.

account which I have heard of these people." The fruit referred to by Herodotus is supposed to have been hemp.

TOBACCO IS DISCOVERED IN THE NEW WORLD

Although Christopher Columbus is generally thought of as the man who discovered America, some modern historians tell us that earlier explorers, among them the Vikings, preceded him to the lands of the western hemisphere. But Columbus regains some of his lost glamour through his authorship of the first accounts of tobacco smoking.

In 1492, while sailing off the coast of Cuba, Columbus, mistakenly believing that he had reached the East Indies, sent ashore two emissaries with letters of introduction to the Khan of Cathay. The Spaniards visited many native villages, but found neither gold nor the Khan of Cathay. They related instead that they had "met with great multitudes of people, men and women, with firebrands in their hands and herbs to smoke, after their custom."

Previously, Columbus also had written in his journal of a friendly offer of tobacco leaves from the natives, as follows:

"Monday, October 25th . . . Being at sea, about midway between Santa Maria and the large island, which I named Fernandina, we met a man in a canoe going from Santa Maria to Fernandina; he had with him a piece of bread which the natives make, as big as one's fist . . . and some dried leaves which are of high value among them, for a quantity of it was brought to me at San Salvador . . ."

But at the time neither Columbus nor his fellow explorers knew what use the Indians made of the dried leaves. Indeed, Columbus not only failed to realize that he had discovered a new continent; he also failed to bring to light the stimulating effects of tobacco and smoking! European explorers did not find out about the pleasures of smoking until several decades later.

Some explorers reported seeing primitive South American Indians smoking through the nose, rather than through the mouth. Many early Indian pipes consisted of Y-shaped forked reeds, hollowed out to receive tobacco. The two ends of the fork were placed in the nostrils and the smoke was inhaled through the nose. This form of smoking is probably more instinctive than smoking through the mouth, since it is our sense of smell that first introduces us to the fragrant aroma of burning tobacco leaves.

Eventually the Indians abandoned nose-smoking and took up smoking through the mouth. The new method was much more convenient, for now the smoker could clamp the pipe between his teeth, leaving both hands free to fill the pipe and light the tobacco.

The Spanish observers related how the Indians would smoke intensely until intoxicated, inhaling the strong smoke through their noses until, numbed and exhausted, they fell asleep. Their womenfolk would then carry the Indians to their hammocks, and leave them lying there until they sobered up.

The word "tobacco" originally did not refer to the leaves or the plant, but rather to the device through which the Indians used to smoke the brown leaves. The Spaniards met many natives smoking dried tobacco rolled inside broad dried leaves of Indian corn. The corn leaves formed a kind of pipe, which the Indians called *tobago* or *tabaco,* a name promptly adopted by the Spaniards. The plant itself and its leaves were called by a variety of names, such as *cohiba, petum, piecelt, yoli,* and *uppowac.* Today, some form of the Spanish term "tabaco," turns up in most languages.

One of the first descriptions of tobacco smoking in the New World reached France through a report of Jacques Cartier, who explored the St. Lawrence River as far as where Montreal, Canada, now stands. In giving his account of the voyage, Cartier describes the Indians' use of tobacco:

"There groweth also a certain kind of herb, whereof in summer they make great provision for all the year, making a great account of it, and only men use it, and first they cause it to be dried in the sun, then wear it about their necks wrapped in a little beast skin, with a hollow piece of stone or wood like a pipe.

"Then when they please they make a powder of it, and then put it in one of the ends of the said pipe, and laying a coal of fire upon it, at the other end suck so long that they fill their bodies full of smoke, till it cometh out of their mouths and nostrils, even as out of a chimney. They say that this doth keep them warm and in health; they never go without some of it about them."

The sixteenth-century French explorer and his fellow-countrymen had little liking for the peppery fumes, and tobacco was not mentioned again in France for another twenty years.

When the conquering Spaniards first witnessed the American Indians puffing violently at smoldering tobacco leaves, they tried it out themselves, and soon fell into the habit of pipe smoking. The sailors then proceeded to carry the practice of pipe smoking back to Europe, where it grew and spread.

The settlers in the new world were quick to exploit the increasing demand for tobacco in Europe, and many British colonists in Virginia made small fortunes in tobacco cultivation. At first, they grew the native North American variety, *Nicotiana rustica,* which they had seen raised by the Indians. But the fortunes of the tobacco growers greatly increased after 1612, when John Rolfe, the husband of the Indian princess, Pocahontas, imported seeds of West Indian tobacco, *Nicotiana tabacum,* to Jamestown. This more desirable variety was an instant success and from then on every British-bound ship leaving the colony carried many bales of tobacco in its hold.

By this time, the value of tobacco had become so universal and so well established that the settlers used it as currency. Some of the colonists, starved for female company in the predominantly male settlements, advertised in England for wives, offering tobacco in payment for their passage. They were willing to deliver one hundred and fifty pounds of tobacco for the passage of each of "a hundred young women of agreeable person and respectable character," making each prospective bride literally worth her weight in tobacco.

JEAN NICOT AND NICOTINE

Much of the early popularity of tobacco in Europe rested on its supposed medicinal properties, rather than on its pleasurable smoking qualities. The tobacco leaf was introduced as a universal remedy for all ailments by a Frenchman, Jean Nicot, from whom both the tobacco plant *Nicotiana* and the term *nicotine* derive their name.

Nicot, appointed ambassador to Portugal by the French Queen, Catherine de Medici, first saw the plant growing in the royal gardens in Lisbon. Learning that the Indians believed the plant to have healing powers, the ambassador decided to experiment. As Nicot's chef happened to have sliced his thumb with a kitchen knife, Nicot bandaged the cut with fresh green tobacco leaves. Surprisingly, the wound healed. A young lady acquaintance of Nicot's had a severe rash on her face, and a gentleman friend had sharp pains in his foot. In both cases, after the application of tobacco leaves, the maladies disappeared.

Nicot pursued his experiments, and not long afterward returned to France where he informed the Queen of the marvelous cures which the plant had effected. One day, when the Queen was suffering from a severe headache, Nicot suggested that she sniff some powder he had crushed from dried tobacco leaves. The Queen agreeably took a pinch of the brown powder, and sneezed. After a few more sneezes, the Queen remembered her headache only to find it considerably improved.

From that moment on, the Queen of France became an ardent snuff enthusiast. The French Court followed her example, and the popularity of tobacco spread throughout the country. For many years the plant was called "The Queen's Herb" or "The Medici's Herb." Even those not suffering from a headache thought they could avoid the risk of getting one by an occasional sniff or two; snuff-taking rapidly became very fashionable.

But snuff was not as yet taken purely for pleasure; it was still considered strictly a medicinal preparation, to be purchased at the local apothecary's. Physicians gave it the somewhat repugnant Latin name of *clysterium nasi* which, liberally translated, means "nasal purge." An encyclopedia published at the time by Nicot himself provides the following listing:

"Nicotiane. A herb with miraculous healing powers against all complaints such as boils, open sores, and rashes, etc. It was introduced to France by the envoy to the King of Portugal, Mr. Jean

Nicot, after whom it derived its name."

The name *Nicotiana* was given to the tobacco plant not by Nicot himself but by the famed Swedish botanist, Linnaeus, to acknowledge Nicot's efforts in encouraging the plant's general use. Nicot did not live to see his medical observations discredited as having little scientific value; nor did he see snuff abused and vulgarized by being taken merely for its pleasurable sensations.

In popularizing snuff, Nicot inadvertently also helped to introduce smoking. A pinch of snuff or a pipe of tobacco both produced a stimulating effect; whether one smoked or took snuff was just a matter of taste. When Frenchmen were first taking snuff, Englishmen were smoking pipes; but later on, when snuff became fashionable in England, pipe smoking had already spread throughout the rest of Europe. After Europe had had sufficient time to try both ways, the taste for smoking triumphed.

TOBACCO IN ENGLAND

The English took to tobacco without regard for the medical attributes which the French credited to it. They found smoking gratifying and enjoyed it for the unique pleasure it afforded. The man who first introduced tobacco to England was the English naval hero Sir John Hawkins, who brought a supply from Florida as early as 1565. The next English sea captain to visit the Western hemisphere, Sir Francis Drake, returned to England from the West Indies in 1573.

It seems incredible to think that in this short period, from 1565 to 1573, the novelty of smoking should have spread so rapidly throughout England. In a medical work published in 1570, the authors state that "within a few years tobacco had become an inmate of England" and describe tobacco smoking as follows:

"You see many sailors, and all those who come back from America, carrying little funnels made from a palm leaf or a reed, in the extreme end of which they insert the rolled and powdered leaves of this plant."

A history of England published a few years later provides the following description of tobacco smoking in the year 1573:

"In these days the taking-in of smoke of the Indian herb called 'Tabaco' by an instrument formed like a little ladle, whereby it passes from the mouth into the head and stomach, is greatly taken-up and used in England . . ."

Although Sir Walter Raleigh did not initiate the use of tobacco into England, he was the man largely responsible for making it fashionable, especially in court circles. He later introduced the tobacco plant and its poor cousin, the potato, to Ireland (the tobacco plant and the potato are botanically related).

Sir Walter, like many other adventurers of the day, enjoyed the gifts which the New World had to offer. He attracted a great deal of attention with his pipe, and made many converts to pipe-smoking. But smoking was still a novelty, and the smoker of that time sometimes suffered at the hands of those who were ignorant of the habit. According to one story, Sir Walter Raleigh happened to employ a new servant, who had never witnessed tobacco smoking. One day, upon entering his master's room, he saw thick columns of smoke emerging from Sir Walter's mouth. Thinking that his master's insides were on fire, he rushed forward, snatched a tankard of beer from the table, and emptied it over Sir Walter's head.

Sir Walter is also the hero of another equally credible story. Although the swashbuckling English explorers and seafarers were very popular with Queen Elizabeth, not one of them had dared to light his pipe in her presence, for it was said that the Queen did not favor the new craze. At last, Sir Walter decided to introduce the pipe into the Royal Chamber. As the Queen's mind could only be changed by indirect and elegant persuasion, Sir Walter devised a subtle tactic.

One day, while in the presence of the Queen, he quietly took out his pipe and began filling it. Before the Queen could object, Sir Walter asked, with a smile, if Her Majesty thought that he could weigh the smoke from his pipe. The Queen could not imagine how this could possibly be done, but Sir Walter offered to perform the feat, and even persuaded the Queen to bet a handful of gold on the outcome.

Sir Walter first asked the Chemist of the Court to bring his most delicate scale. Carefully filling his pipe, he placed it on the scale, and asked the Chemist to note its weight. Sir Walter then settled down to a comfortable smoke while the Queen and her courtiers watched attentively. When he had finished, he left the ashes in the pipe which was once more weighed by the Chemist.

Sir Walter then turned to the Queen and said: "If the present weight of the pipe is subtracted from its weight before I started smoking, the difference must be the weight of that which has disappeared, that is, Your Majesty, the weight of the smoke."

The Queen graciously conceded the point and gave Sir Walter the promised handful of gold coins, saying: "I have met many alchemists who have let gold go up in smoke, but only you, Sir Walter, have I seen transmute smoke into gold." With that remark, pipe smoking was officially introduced into Queen Elizabeth's court, and in fashionable circles throughout England.

Sir Walter always remained a heavy smoker, and later in his life, after he had lost his popularity at court and was imprisoned in the Tower of London, his pipe became a comforting companion in his lonely cell.

Chapter 2

The Briar and the Meerschaum:– King and Queen of Pipes

THE BRIAR justly may be called the king of pipes. It has displaced almost every other kind of pipe from the smoker's shelf. And rightly so, for briarwood is ideal pipe material—hard, tough and fire-resistant. Moreover, the briar pipe gives a cool, sweet, mellow smoke for many years.

Similarly, the lovely white meerschaum may be called the queen of pipes. It is delicate, beautiful, and when carefully handled yields a gentle, sweet smoke.

THE INVENTION OF THE MEERSCHAUM PIPE

The meerschaum pipe made its debut in the tobacco world about 100 years before the discovery of the briar burl. Until the meerschaum came into use, clay pipes were the average man's smoke.

According to an old story, it was pure chance that led to the utilization of meerschaum for pipe bowls. It seems that in the year 1720 there lived in Budapest, Hungary, a shoemaker named Karl Kovacs, who was also a talented carver. One day a member of Budapest society, Count Andrassy, brought Kovacs two white lumps of a strange mineral which the Count had found while traveling in the Near East. The Count wondered if the cobbler could carve some artistic design out of the material, as yet unnamed. Kovacs examined the white lumps carefully, and it struck him that the light, porous mineral would be ideal for a pipe bowl.

23

Being a heavy smoker, the Count readily agreed to the suggestion.

Kovacs fashioned each lump into the shape of a bowl, gave one to the Count, and kept the other one for himself. After giving his bowl a trial smoke, Kovacs noticed that some parts of the white mineral had turned a golden brown. The brown spots were the prints of his fingers, which had been coated with cobbler's wax. In a burst of inspiration, he waxed the rest of the bowl, and watched with satisfaction as the golden color spread evenly over the entire surface. Soon both Kovacs and Count Andrassy had the pleasure of smoking lovely, golden-brown meerschaum pipes.

The demand for Kovacs's pipes quickly grew, and the shoemaker had less and less time left for his cobbling. It was commonly said that Kovacs literally carved gold out of meerschaum with his tools. His maiden pipe, created for Count Andrassy, was awarded a place of honor in the pipe collection of the National Museum in Budapest.

For a century, from 1750 to 1850, hand-carved meerschaum pipes were too costly for the average pipe smoker. Only the wealthy could afford to purchase a block of meerschaum and engage some famous artist to carve the pipe. The pipes were fitted with pure amber stems, and were quite properly regarded as true works of art.

As meerschaum pipe carving became a profitable business, determined efforts were made to uncover new deposits of the mineral. Finally, a meerschaum pipe boom began, lasting up to the end of the Nineteenth Century. During this period, numerous Austrian factories, employing hundreds of carvers, turned out thousands upon thousands of handsomely shaped meerschaum pipes.

Although meerschaum may be found in many parts of the world, the highest grade, perhaps the only "true," meerschaum comes from Asia Minor, and almost entirely from Turkey. Since the mineral is quite soft and easily shaped, meerschaum has been a popular carving substance in Turkey for many centuries. Beads and other art objects cut from meerschaum can be found in Turkish museums, an indication that the white substance has been known and employed for a long time. But the use of meerschaum for pipes had to await the discovery of tobacco and the introduction of the mineral into Europe.

The term "meerschaum" is composed of two German words, *meer,* meaning "sea," and *schaum,* meaning "foam." The white, porous mineral is so light that when dry it will float on water. The story is that a piece of the material once actually was observed floating on the waves and, since it resembled real sea foam, was dubbed "meerschaum."

Meerschaum also has a more scientific chemical name, hydrous magnesium silicate, with its usual formula being the rather formidable $H_4Mg_2Si_3O_{10}$. The geologic origin of the mineral remains a mystery. One theory states that meerschaum consists at least in part of prehistoric sea shells, remnants decomposed and fused into meerschaum over millions of years.

When meerschaum deposits lie near the surface of the ground, they can be uncovered with an ordinary miner's pick. If the deposits are more deeply buried, they are dug from open pits and galleries about twenty-five feet in depth. In Turkey, where meerschaum has been mined for almost a thousand years, more than 20,000 pits have already been exhausted and abandoned.

When the meerschaum "stones," as they are called, are removed from the ground in their natural state, they are covered with clay of a brownish-gray color. Fortunately, such a stone is much heavier than the finished meerschaum block which eventually will give birth to a pipe.

Workmen then clean the meerschaum, using special knives to remove both the clay and damaged portions. At this point the stones appear as white, uneven lumps, marked with grooves and clefts. They are rough-sanded and shaped into blocks. The form varies with each individual block, for none of the precious material is wasted if it can possibly be saved.

Next comes one of the most important steps—the drying process. Since the mineral is normally quite damp when dug from the ground, its moisture must be removed. This is achieved by drying it in low-temperature ovens for several weeks. An inspector then examines each block for flaws or irregularities. After the inspector's knife eliminates the weak spots, a large block may be cut into two or three smaller blocks. Each block is then sanded once more and buffed to a high polish.

The meerschaum is now ready to be graded. Experts with many years of experience classify the stones according to size, weight, color, homogeneity, texture, shape, and other qualities. There are in all five main categories of meerschaum, and twelve qualities to be checked in each group, making a grand total of sixty different grades!

These main categories bear the exotic Turkish names of Siramali, Birmbirlik, Pamuklu, Daneli, and Ortodokme. These correspond, respectively, to the Viennese classifications of Lager, Grosse Baumwolle, Kleine Baumwolle, Polierte Kasten, and Geputz.

After classification, the meerschaum blocks are shipped to all parts of the world for the next step. Meerschaum pipes are not usually carved in Turkey. More often the blocks are fashioned into pipes by Old World craftsmen. In their heyday, meerschaum pipe factories jealously guarded their trade secrets. After the meerschaum blocks were received at the factory, they were graded according to quality, with the best pieces going to the most skillful carvers.

If the meerschaum had become hardened by exposure to air, it was softened by soaking it in water for half an hour. The pipe then went to a "rougher" who carved its rough outlines. A second artisan shaved off the rough edges, drilled the bowl and shank, and made any final cuts required. The pipe then was passed into the hands of a master craftsman, who carved an appropriate design.

Some carvers liked to work on the meerschaum only while it was soft. This meant soaking the pipe in water every so often to prevent it from drying out. A thorough waxing completed the job, and the pipe was ready for the market.

Today, the manufacture of meerschaum pipes remains essentially the same as a hundred years ago. After carving, the pipes are placed in a drying room for about fifteen hours.

The pipes are then ready for the delicate job of polishing. Special substances such as dried bull-rushes (a kind of grass) are used as the polishing medium, since the soft and porous meerschaum surface cannot stand even the finest jeweler's abrasives. The tedious polishing process is carried out partly by machine and partly by hand, and takes several days.

To help the smoker more speedily bring out the rich yellow color found in long-smoked meerschaum pipes, the new pipes are soaked in boiling beeswax. The wax seals the porous mineral, will retain the yellow color of the tobacco juices, and gives the pipe an attractive glossy finish.

At this point, the pipe is finished, but not yet ready for the customer. A special case or box must be furnished for each pipe for its protection.

In the past, the stems of all meerschaum pipes were made of that rich golden-yellow substance, amber. Today, when an amber pipe stem costs about five dollars per inch, other materials are used. The stems still are yellow in color, however, since this tint has long been associated with meerschaum pipes.

Meerschaums, renowned for their cool, mellow smoke, remain very popular today. But the beautiful hand-carved examples have all but disappeared into the hands of collectors and museums.

Follow the manufacturer's instructions carefully when breaking in a meerschaum pipe. As the pipe is smoked, its color will turn slowly from pure white to rich, creamy golden-yellow; continued smoking will eventually turn it to a beautiful autumn brown. At this point, the meerschaum reaches its full ripe quality and flavor. The smoker can then reap his due reward for the care required during the long breaking-in period.

Properly handled, a meerschaum will last many years and give its owner innumerable hours of enjoyable smoking. It actually improves with age, and the longer it is smoked, the sweeter and mellower it becomes. The smoker who owns a meerschaum pipe is always proud of it, and no man who does not have at least one genuine meerschaum in his possession can be called a true lover of pipes.

THE DISCOVERY OF THE BRIAR BURL

Some years after the introduction of the meerschaum pipe, smokers began to realize that the best material for pipe bowls was wood—of a very special kind. Clay, porcelain, and meerschaum, despite their admirable qualities, were too fragile; metal pipes, while sturdy, heated rapidly and were too heavy. Pipes carved from cherry- and willow-wood, however, met with little success. The creation of the ideal pipe, the universal pipe, had to await the discovery of the briar.

The introduction of briarwood as pipe material was quite accidental. It was linked to the cult of hero worship which sprang up shortly after the death in 1821 of the French emperor, Napoleon Bonaparte. One of those who glorified the emperor's memory was a French pipe maker, who decided to honor his hero by making a pilgrimage to the Mediterranean island of Corsica, Napoleon's birthplace.

Being a passionate smoker, the pipe maker took one of his most beautiful meerschaum pipes with him. In an unlucky moment, however, he broke the bowl of his pipe, and was left without means of smoking. Fortunately, in that same Corsican village there lived a farmer known for his skill in carving. The Frenchman promptly commissioned the farmer to carve a new pipe for him out of any suitable wood.

The farmer soon presented the the pipe maker with an attractive pipe, made of a hard, close-grained, pale golden wood. The pipe had so many fine qualities that its owner brought back to France several specimens of the wood from which it was made—the burl of the tree-heath, or *bruyere,* as it is called in French. Eventually the name "bruyere" was anglicized, first into "bruyer," then "brier," and later, "briar."

Enthusiastic over his discovery, the pipe maker brought his briar samples to St. Claude, a small French town from whose factory he usually bought his wooden pipe stems. This town, located in a remote valley of the Jura mountains, had a remarkable history as a center of wood-carving.

The craft had been introduced to St. Claude during the Middle Ages by monks, to while away the long winter months when heavy mountain snowfalls kept both people and livestock indoors. At the great Abbey, the center of the medieval settlement, the monks carved rosaries, crucifixes, and ordinary household goods out of boxwood, which grew abundantly in the neighborhood. The peasants began to imitate the monks, and wood-carving soon became the chief occupation of the inhabitants. The former monastery grew into a thriving town; its ancient Abbey church became a cathedral.

The French pipe manufacturer asked the clever craftsmen of St. Claude to try their hand at the new material by carving out some pipe bowls. The artisans soon found that the briar presented some problems; the wood had to pass through a complex seasoning process before it could be fashioned into satisfactory pipes. Also, the knotted and gnarled briar burls were all different, and contained many flaws. It took a good deal of experience to learn to make the proper cuts so as to carve the blocks to advantage.

Despite these difficulties, the briar pipe industry developed and took hold in St. Claude, eventually dwarfing all the other carved goods manufactured in that town. A century after the discovery of the briar root, 5,000 inhabitants of St. Claude were busy turning out some 30,000,000 pipes a year. Thus the broken meerschaum pipe bowl in Corsica led to the foundation of a new and thriving business. Briar pipe making spread from France to England and then to America, and the briar root quickly eclipsed all other pipe materials.

THE BRIAR PLANT

The briar plant is a tough little tree which the botanists call *Erica Arborea,* a member of the heather family. It closely resembles a dwarf tree, since it grows to no more than fifteen to twenty feet high.

Found chiefly on the shores of the Mediterranean basin, its development depends on climate and soil. Most plants flourish readily under abundant rainfall and in fertile soil. But the briar most suitable for use in pipes is that which has to fight for its survival high in the mountainous Mediterranean country. There the soil is barren and rocky, rainfall is sparse, and growing conditions are among the worst in the world. Harsh winds tear at the hardy plant; the rocky soil resists its efforts to grow. But the hardy briar drives its roots into the smallest crevices, forcing the soil or rock apart bit by bit.

In fighting for a foothold in the arid soil so that it can nourish itself and grow, the little shrub develops a tight, hard-grained knob of wood just above its roots. This toughest portion of the plant, the briar burl, makes the briar plant unique in the plant kingdom, at least insofar as pipe smokers are concerned.

The burl found in most fully-grown briar bushes lies just below the surface of the earth, barely covered with dirt. Neither stem nor root, the burl is the meeting place of the roots which grow downward from it, and the trunk which grows upward from it. In fact, the burl serves as the briar's shield against an unfriendly environment; it forces an opening in the hard rock or soil above the roots and anchors the plant against the wind that would bend or break it. Only the burl, often erroneously called the briar "root," is used in making briar pipes.

The frail-looking briar plant hardly seems like a promising

A briar root   The heath tree from which the briar
                      root is derived

candidate for hard, fire-resistant pipe bowls. The bush boasts little foliage, and its branches tend to cluster around the spindly trunk, seemingly for protection against the elements. But its sparse foliage and feeble branches encourage the growth of the burl just under the ground. If the climate were more temperate, the foliage might be more beautiful, but the burls from which pipes are made would be smaller and less desirable.

Until quite recently, most briarwood was obtained from the rocky deserts of Algeria. Today, however, much of the high-quality briar comes from Spain, Corsica, Sardinia, Sicily, Greece, and Asia Minor. In these regions a mild winter with occasional showers is usually followed by a hot, dry summer. In trying to survive the period of drought, the briar develops its characteristic close, hard grain. These areas also furnish the arid, infertile soil from which the best briar burls are derived. Briar grown in more fertile soil has fewer flaws than that which comes from the rocky mountain country. But since a hard briar is most desirable, a flawless piece of mountain briar has a higher value than a flawless, but softer, briar block from a fertile valley.

Good briar burls are difficult to find. The large heath shrubs take a long time to mature; the most suitable root may be sixty to one hundred years old. Some of the finest briar burls ever found may have been growing for as long as 250 years. If the briar grows in remote and desolate areas, such as the rocky woodlands of Sardinia, the heavy burls must be carried by hand or by mule over rough mountain paths.

Because of the dry climate, forest fires may quickly sweep over a tract of briar. The area then becomes useless for fifty years or more, until another growth of briar has had the time to mature. Moreover, sparks falling on an exposed burl may pit the wood and lay it open to destructive insect pests. If the briar continues to grow, it will close around the cavity, and the flaw will not become apparent until the burl is cut, or perhaps not even until the pipe itself receives its finishing cuts.

Because of the long growth period, it is somewhat easier to seek out natural briar than to try and cultivate it. Large areas of virgin 100-year-old briar forests have been opened up in Greece in recent years. In areas where the briar bushes are carefully cultivated, however, sections of young burls may be removed every three or four years, leaving enough of the plant alive for another cutting, three or four years later.

The briar root made its entry at the crucial moment in the history of smoking. At the time, the pipe faced two increasingly powerful competitors, the cigar and cigarette, and as a result was declining in popular favor. But the introduction of briarwood allowed pipe manufacturers to produce a small, hard-wearing pipe —handy, attractive, and relatively inexpensive.

The briar pipe put the luxury of fine pipe smoking within the reach of every man's wallet, and the briar pipe has now become as popular as the clay pipe once was.

Chapter 3

Pipe Varieties

FOR SERIOUS PIPE-SMOKING, the briar should always be your first choice. However, if on occasion you desire a novel experience, try reaching for one of the more unusual pipes, such as a clay pipe, a calabash, a corncob, a churchwarden, or even a water pipe. These are some of the most readily available types, although the variety of possible pipes and pipe materials must be counted as almost endless.

Smokers throughout the world have at one time or another used pipes made of bamboo, bone, bronze, glass, horn, iron, ivory (both walrus and elephant), nutshells, silver, steel, and stone, to name but a few. Most of these pipe materials would give a disappointing smoke. However, modern pipe smokers have found that a few of the more unusual pipe types do provide a satisfactory smoke, and add diversity to the smoker's shelf as well.

THE CALABASH

The calabash pipe is made from the neck of a gourd, a plant whose family includes the cucumber, the melon, and the squash.

The gourds from which these pipes are fashioned usually come from South Africa, where the calabash originated. When the Dutch founded Cape Town in 1652, they discovered the natives busily smoking hemp in homemade gourd pipes. The natives would clean out the gourd, let it dry thoroughly, and then use it, as a pipe.

Calabash pipes became popular because they are beautiful and of an unusual shape. The calabash gourd makes an ideal pipe

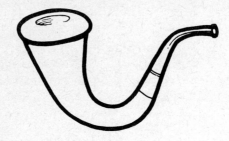

The calabash pipe

because of its light weight, its large air space, which yields a cool smoke, and its tendency to color well.

After being cut, the gourd is usually fitted with a meerschaum insert, called a "cup" or "top bowl." Since nature forms the gourd, no two calabash pipes are ever exactly alike, and each pipe must be hand-made. The meerschaum insert is fitted into a cork ring to insure air-tight connection. The connection between the shank and the curved vulcanite stem also calls for careful hand fitting.

While a gourd is growing, the cultivator aids in the formation of its gracefully curved neck by gradually training the neck to the correct form. This is done by placing under the gourd a flat board in which pegs are inserted, pegs that hold the neck in a prescribed position. These pegs are then moved, little by little, so as to force the neck into the curve desired.

After the gourd is harvested and its neck removed, the flesh inside the neck is scraped away. The outside of the gourd is then sanded and polished with fine abrasive, and the gourd is dried in the sun. Only then is it fitted with stem and bowl.

The large air space beneath the bowl cools the smoke and prevents juices from entering the stem and the smoker's mouth.

Indeed, the graceful, lightweight calabash provides one of the coolest smokes possible—and its unique shape makes it an ideal reading or fireside pipe.

CORNCOBS

Washington, Missouri, is the home of the corncob pipe. Washington resembles any other small town on the banks of the Missouri River except that it turns out about 15,000,000 pipes a year, all made of corncobs. The corncob-pipe industry has helped support farmers in the area ever since 1869, when a local farmer first thought of the lowly corncob as a cheap, expendable, and available pipe material.

Over the years, local farmers have developed a special type of corn, known as "Collier" corn, with an exceptionally large and firm cob. The plant is large, the stalk measuring two inches in diameter and taking one hundred and twenty days to mature instead of the usual ninety. The farmers bring the cobs to the pipe factory and sell the kernels separately.

Before the cobs can be worked, they have to dry for at least two years. Cobs smaller than two inches in diameter are rejected. The outside of each cob is smoothed out by machine; the soft spots are filled with plaster of Paris, fitted with a stem or reed, and varnished. The modern corncob has many different bowl finishes and a variety of shanks and stems.

The corncob pipe should be smoked slowly and allowed to dry thoroughly between smokes, to give many months, or even years, of pleasant smoking. As with any type of pipe, the smoker should have several and smoke them in rotation.

There are as many corncob-pipe styles as there are styles of briar pipes. Some smokers prefer corncobs to all other pipe materials except briar. In general, corncobs make a satisfying change-of-pace pipe and provide a pleasant diversion.

WATER PIPES

The idea of forcing smoke through water before allowing it to enter the mouth was probably originated by the African Bushmen or Pygmies. Many years before Columbus discovered the New World, these natives were already smoking hemp in a variety of water pipes, such as gourds, hollowed-out sections of wooden logs, horns of animals, and sections of bamboo.

THE NARGHILE PIPE AND HOW IT WORKS

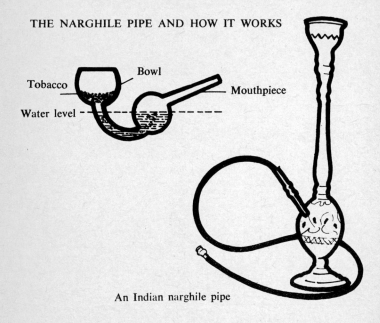

An Indian narghile pipe

But the most practical vessel for holding water seems to have been the coconut shell, because it was hard and durable. Where it might have taken days to hollow out a log, a coconut shell could be turned into a pipe in a matter of minutes, and would last for many years.

This water pipe, also known as the *narghile,* a word that means "coconut shell," was often fitted with a pair of reed or bamboo tubes, one to hold the burning tobacco and the other to draw the smoke through.

Today, water pipes remain very popular throughout Africa, the Near East, and the Far East, where they are known under the diverse names of *narghile* (Indian), *hookah* (Turkish), *kalian*

(Persian), *hubble-bubble,* and many others.

The best-known Persian or Turkish type of water pipe generally consists of a jar that holds the water and a long tube, one end supporting the burning tobacco and the other end extending into the jar below the level of the water. A second tube, above the water level, is used to draw the smoke downward from the bowl, through the water, and into the smoker's mouth.

The smoke of the water pipe is cooler than that of any other pipe. By the time the smoke has bubbled through the water and passed out of the long tube, it attains nearly room temperature.

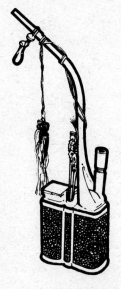

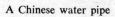
A Chinese water pipe

Papuan pipes smoked by the
natives of New Guinea

The smoke also becomes very mild. The water acts as a filter which keeps the impurities, tobacco flakes and moisture particles from entering the mouth. But the water also absorbs some of the taste and flavor.

If you have the inclination to smoke a water pipe, you can probably find a Turkish, Persian, Indian, or all-metal Chinese water pipe in many good pipe shops. You can vary the taste of the smoke by adding different flavorings to the water; the possible aromas that can be created are without end.

The water receptacle should be rinsed out after every three or four smokes, and the tube which holds the tobacco bowl should be cleaned or replaced at regular intervals. Make sure that all the fittings connecting the tubes and jar are air-tight. The water pipe is a cool and agreeable departure from ordinary pipes, ideal for relaxed, hot-weather smoking.

CLAY PIPES

Millions of clay pipes were smoked in the seventeenth and early eighteenth centuries, especially in England, where they greatly

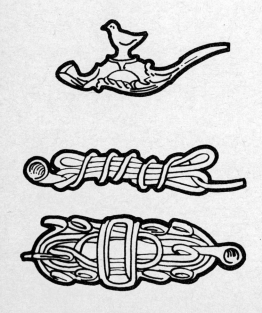

English Staffordshire-ware pipes

increased the popularity of smoking. The pipes were so inexpensive that they could be discarded after one or two smokes, and replaced by fresh pipes. The clay churchwarden, one of the most popular clay pipes ever created, has been immortalized in art and literature and remains a favorite.

Clay pipes are still largely handmade, from good-quality clay. Wet clay is placed in metal pipe molds, with a long steel needle running through the stems to shape the air holes. The pipes are then dried, kiln-baked, and finished. Bowl decorations may be transferred from the mold, or painted on.

The city of Gouda, in the Netherlands, is the traditional clay-pipe center of the world. Even today, Gouda factories are turning out about 20,000 clay pipes daily, or about 7,000,000 pipes a year, conclusive evidence that the clay pipe has remained a popular item.

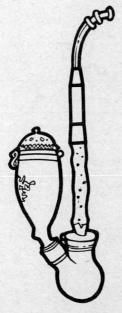

Alsatian porcelain pipe

The list of pipes available to the more imaginative smoker does not end here. Pipes with an aluminum shank and bowl base, briar bowl, and vulcanite stem are popular today. They are simple to clean—the bowl can be easily removed and the shank scoured thoroughly with boiling water.

Wooden pipes with porcelain bowls were widely smoked in Germany in the nineteenth century, and are still enjoyed by many pipe smokers. Long-stemmed pipes have also waxed and waned in popularity over the years. The churchwarden style, popular in clay and metal in the sixteenth and seventeenth centuries, has recently been revived in a somewhat shorter-stemmed briar version. The long-stemmed Turkish *chibouque* remains a favorite of smokers who like to puff while sitting cross-legged on a cushion.

Whatever your style of smoking, chances are that somewhere you'll find a pipe to match it.

Chapter 4

Selecting Your Pipe

SELECTING YOUR PIPE is a very personal affair. The pipe must, first of all, fit your personality and character. It should also enhance your appearance, and provide you with the comfort, confidence, and satisfaction to which every pipe smoker is entitled.

When selecting a pipe, regard it as the old friend it will become, as something you will be living with for many years.

Once you've decided on the pipe style that suits you best, you will want to make sure that the pipe is of good quality and correctly priced. Judging the merits of a pipe requires a certain knowledge of pipe manufacture, a familiarity with briarwood, and a smattering of background in the economics of the pipe industry.

This chapter will serve as a general guide to briar pipe selection. It is designed to help you choose a quality briar, and to tell you how much you should pay for it. It would also be a good idea to glance at *Chapter Seven,* "How Briar Pipes Are Made," before actually choosing your pipe.

FLAWS AND WHAT THEY MEAN

To make certain that you get the best pipe for your money, select a reliable pipe dealer who sells the product of a well-known pipe-maker. In this way, you can be assured of a quality pipe, since the manufacturer's reputation depends on the excellence of the pipe bearing his name.

Because briar is a product of nature, imperfections occasionally occur in the burl. The skilled pipe maker eliminates or minimizes such flaws, however, through careful selection of briar block and hand-finishing of the bowl. These minute imperfections in no way affect the smoking quality of the pipe, and painstaking hand-finishing makes the flaws invisible to the naked eye.

Thus, pipes which may at first seem identical may vary sharply in cost, one selling for ten dollars and the other for only three. The reason for the wide difference is usually that the less expensive pipe has an imperfection or two, while the other pipe may have no visible faults at all.

A pipe with a crack penetrating the entire bowl would be useless, and no reputable pipe maker would allow it to carry his name. Neither you nor anyone else would want it at any price. However, a good pipe with one or more minute surface imperfections, rendered invisible to the naked eye, will give you as fine a smoke for as long a time as a perfect pipe. Finally, you may run across an outstanding specimen, a pipe with beautiful grain, and not a visible defect inside or outside the bowl.

Imperfections originate in the briar burl when the growth of the burl is interrupted in some way. One kind of defect may be caused by a strong wind that bends or twists the plant so that its roots grow in an abnormal manner. This, in turn, may form small air pockets, partially open or completely enclosed . . . and invisible unless the pipe-maker's cutting blade happens to slice through one and expose it.

Another type of fault occurs when a small stone becomes embedded in the burl and the plant continues to grow around it. Such a stone, like the air pocket, remains undetected until the pipe is shaped from the wood. If the stone is not too deeply lodged within the briar block, it can be gouged out.

A flaw may also develop if water somehow becomes trapped inside the briar burl. The end result is a small pit or air hole in the finished pipe.

Blemishes are seldom visible on the surface of the briar block.

Indeed, the manufacturer can never be sure that a particular block will yield a perfect pipe until the pipe is finished. Even the final sandpapering, which removes a mere thousandth of an inch from the wood, may disclose a hidden fault of such dimensions that the pipe has to be discarded. More often, the pipe maker will cut into an expensive block of the finest briar and find a few tiny flaws. These defects will be too small for the briar to be scraped, but large enough to relegate the pipe to the bargain counter.

The finer pipes, of course, never possess a single visible flaw. This is the result of careful selection. Reputable pipe makers sell their less-than-perfect pipes as "seconds" to dealers who market the pipes under different brand names. Very often an inexpensive pipe may appear perfect to the untrained eye; yet it will probably have a very small defect which may escape your scrutiny but not that of the inspector at the factory.

Do faults affect the smoking quality of the pipe? The answer depends upon where the flaw is located. If it is on the outside of the pipe bowl, reasonably small, and not too deep, chances are it will have no effect on the pipe's smoking properties. But if the defect is on the inside of the bowl, beware! Such flaws eventually lead to trouble.

Imperfections on the inside of the bowl appear as rough spots, depressions, or holes in the bowl wall. Unless the pipe is carefully broken in and a thick cake maintained over the bad spot, a burn-out could occur. The wood around the flaw may scorch easily, adversely affecting the pipe for smoking purposes.

Many smokers refuse to buy pipes with a carved finish because they believe that the manufacturer has used the carving process to eliminate faults on the outside of the pipe. This assumption is not necessarily true. When a defect shows up during the pipe-making process, the manufacturer has two alternatives (if he does not wish to discard the pipe): he can give the pipe a carved finish and remove the flaw in the process, or he can reduce the outside diameter of the bowl, leaving a smooth finish, and also removing the blemish.

In either case, the result is a flaw-free pipe. Many pipe smokers prefer a carved pipe because of its original appearance, lighter weight, and cooler smoke. The carving increases the surface area of the bowl, which in turn results in a greater dispersal of heat.

PIPE SHAPES

There are several principal pipe-bowl designs which the experienced smoker will readily recognize, plus a half dozen variations on each familiar type. The following are the more common pipe-bowl shapes:

The *pot* bowl has parallel sides at right angles to the shank, with the base of the bowl slightly rounded. The pot bowl is usually larger than most other shapes. If the height of the bowl measures less than its diameter, it presents a somewhat squat appearance, and is referred to as a *squat pot*. Similarly, if the bowl's height is equal to or larger than its diameter, it is called a *large* or *raised pot,* respectively. The *pot bowl setler* shape has a pot bowl with a flat base.

The *Dublin* bowl diverges from the base of the bowl to its rim, like an upright letter V. On the other hand, the outline of the *prince* bowl converges from base to rim, as an inverted V. The *billiard, pear,* and *apple* bowls all bulge outward.

Traditionally, special names have been given to various pipe styles that combine certain shapes of bowl and shank. The *Bull Moose,* for example, is a sturdy pipe with a full, short, round shank, an apple bowl, and a slightly curved stem. The *Woodstock* has a Dublin bowl, a slightly curved stem, and an oval shank.

The *Bulldog* has a pear bowl with a paneled (flattened) top, is beaded (grooved) around the circumference of the bowl, and has a diamond-shaped shank and stem. Straight shanks of greater than average length, with oval or round cross-sections, are called *Canadian.*

The *Oom Paul* is a large pipe, usually measuring about two and one-half inches from the rim of the bowl to the bottom. It got its name from "Oom" Paul Kruger, the Boer leader during the South African war at the dawn of this century. Although the diameter of the bowl is that of an ordinary pipe, it is very deep and holds a great deal of tobacco.

The *Dawes* pipe (more correctly named the *Lyons,* after its inventor, Charles Herbert Lyons) happened to be the favorite pipe of General Charles G. Dawes, Vice-President of the United States from 1925 to 1929. General Dawes smoked the curious pipe incessantly and it became popularly known as the *Dawes Underslung,* because the shank joined the bowl near its rim.

CHART OF PIPE SHAPES

SLIM APPLE

WOODSTOCK

LARGE DUBLIN

BILLIARD

LOVAT

LARGE POT BOWL

TAPER BULLDOG

LIVERPOOL

PANEL

EGG

SADDLE BIT BULLDOG

CANADIAN

SLIM BILLIARD

FOUR SQUARE

GIANT BILLIARD

OOM-PAUL

PRINCE

LIGHT BULLDOG

BENT

SADDLE-BIT DUBLIN

APPLE

End View

CHUBBY

SADDLE POT BOWL

SETTER

RHODESIAN

Top View

WELL

OVAL BOWL

TOPPER

AUTHOR

End View

ENGLISH SADDLE

SCOTCH PUG

PEAR

SLIM SADDLE
APPLE

SADDLE APPLE

BULL MOOSE

STEM SHAPES

Most smokers buying a new pipe examine the bowl with care, but rarely do more than glance at the stem. Although the stem of a pipe may have little effect on the quality of the smoke, it largely determines whether the pipe will feel comfortable or awkward, and whether it will appear beautifully proportioned or odd-shaped and clumsy.

Walk into any pipe shop and chances are that you'll find at least thirty different pipe-stem designs. Stem manufacturers have designed their stems to bring out the graceful qualities of the bowl so that the finished pipe has a conformation pleasing to the eye, and a balance that makes the pipe easy to hold in one's mouth. Stems are classified by number and are always measured in millimeters.

Thus each pipe shape traditionally incorporates a certain style of stem especially suited to the bowl, in terms both of beauty and

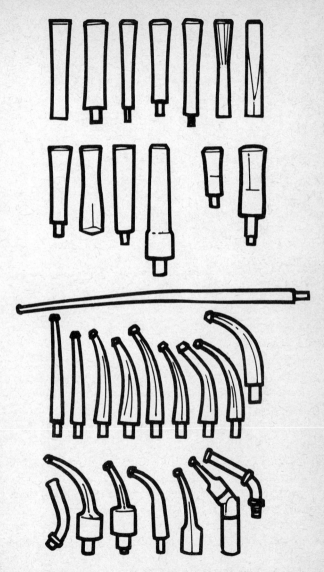

Pipe stems are designed to bring out the graceful qualities of the pipe bowl. Here are but a few of the many stems that are currently in use.

53

the smoker's comfort. A Canadian shape, for example, with its long wooden shank, would not look very well-proportioned with a long stem. Consequently, the Canadian is usually found with a short stem.

Large pipes with short shanks must have longer stems to keep the bowl and shank-stem line in proportion. A churchwarden would, of course, require a very long, slender stem. Bulldogs with diamond-shaped shanks need matching diamond-shaped stems. In the Oom Paul shape, the stem must be bent to a full right angle in order to keep the bowl upright and allow the bit to rest comfortably between the smoker's teeth.

Most bowl shapes can be fitted with a variety of stem shapes, but not all stem shapes fit all bowl shapes. Manufacturers usually select the correct stems for their pipes, but in the end the customer must be the one to choose a stem which seems both comfortable and beautiful to him.

FILTERS

Many modern pipes come with an aluminum filter built into the stem. The filter has a double purpose. It lengthens the path the smoke must travel before entering the mouth so as to cool the smoke, and also so as to prevent small particles of tobacco, tars, and nicotine from reaching the lips. Filters do trap much of the undesirable matter such as tars and oils, and many ideas on the subject have been developed over the years. This is demonstrated by the innumerable filter designs registered every year with the U.S. Patent Office.

A number of pipes on the market are equipped with chemical filters, cloth filters, or more complicated filters of aluminum tubing. Some smokers may find that such filters suit their taste, but to most pipe lovers a simple aluminum stem filter, or no filter at all, usually proves desirable.

PIPE AND PERSONALITY

When selecting a pipe, try to find a shape or style in keeping with your own particular character. Or, if you must, choose a pipe so outstanding as to attract favorable attention. Sherlock Holmes, the fictitious detective created by Sir Arthur Conan Doyle, is almost as famous for his calabash as for his powers of reasoning. Mark Twain, by contrast, preferred a rough-hewn corncob, and puffed furiously away while writing. It is said that he burned his pipes out so frequently that he had to employ a man to break them in for him.

One way to find out whether or not a pipe flatters you is to pose with it before a mirror. Try on the pipe as you would try on a hat or an overcoat. If the pipe looks out of place in your mouth, put it back on the shelf and try another one.

A big man, over six feet tall and weighing two hundred pounds, would look ridiculous smoking a midget briar. On the other hand, a small skinny fellow has no business smoking a pipe nearly as large as his face.

Generally, a tall slender man looks better smoking a straight, long-stemmed pipe, such as the lumberman or billiard. Short, plump men, with rounder faces, look more natural with curved pipes such as the bent or Oom Paul. But the ultimate choice is up to the smoker, whose own taste should guide his selection.

People who work with their hands usually prefer pipes with short stems. Short stems allow greater freedom of movement than other shapes. Long-stemmed pipes, such as the lumberman or Canadian, are best suited for leisure-time smoking.

If a pipe is destined for easy-chair smoking, you might like to select a calabash or a meerschaum. A heavy briar also rates as a good choice if the pipe does not have to be carried about, since a weighty bowl usually provides a cooler smoke than a light bowl.

For leisurely reading or conversation, a long-stemmed pipe ranks high, for the smoke will not get into the smoker's eyes. This does not mean that long-stemmed pipes can be carried between the teeth; on the contrary, the longer the stem, the harder it is to hold the pipe upright. If you must keep your pipe in your mouth at all times, you'll find a short pipe much more suitable.

A pipe with a curved stem is even better suited for carrying between the teeth. A curved pipe hangs downward, producing

55

less leverage on the teeth, and may even rest against the smoker's chin. A pipe to be smoked out of doors should be fitted with a cap. The cap will prevent flying ashes from starting small fires and keep the wind from burning the tobacco so rapidly as to cause a cracked bowl. Pipe caps come in various sizes, to fit any size bowl.

PIPE PRICES

A first-quality pipe is a thing of beauty, a cherished possession—the end result of age-old skills and artistry combined with fine old briar. It has no visible defects. Its bore runs true down the center of the shank and enters the bowl at the bottom center point. If, in addition to all of this, a briar has an outstandingly close grain that runs straight up and down the bowl, it probably will sell for fifteen dollars or more. In making one's choice, grain and flawlessness are the standards by which briar pipes are judged.

Most manufacturers find that out of one hundred pipes, perhaps only five can be rated as of the first quality. These flawless, straight-grained specimens naturally fetch a top price. Pipes of less demanding standards may be sold under the manufacturer's name at a lower price, or they may be sold under another trade name. Slightly defective pipes of good grain, as well as cheaper pipes, called "seconds," which have many plugged or smoothed-over flaws, may sell for a couple of dollars or less. The price of quality pipes is based strictly on the law of supply and demand; there are few pipes of high quality but many low-grade pipes of inferior quality.

Many novice smokers choose a cheap pipe of inferior grade as their first selection, with the intention of obtaining a better pipe as soon as they learn the art of smoking. This turns out to be poor reasoning. The smoker will find that it simply does not pay to buy pipes of inferior quality as such pipes do not possess the same smoking qualities as fine pipes and may discourage any further attempts at pipe smoking.

Top-quality pipes sell for five dollars and up. Other pipes of good quality are available at prices below five dollars. The price of the pipe depends on many things—the perfection of the grain pattern, the age of the briar employed, the trueness of the shape, the finish, the quality of the vulcanite stem, the absence of surface imperfections, to name the most important. Here again, the best guarantee of a pipe's true value resides in the reliability of the dealer and the integrity of the pipe maker. As in other handmade items created from a product of nature, the price of a briar pipe is based on quality and workmanship.

Don't count on the chance of finding a bargain pipe; pay a little more and get your money's worth of pipe-smoking pleasure. If you pay five dollars or more for a pipe from a reputable manufacturer, you will be guaranteed a reasonably good pipe which will give you a fine smoke for many years.

Chapter 5

Selecting Your Tobacco

IN THE DAYS when America was merely a group of colonies, and tobacco smoking was still in its infancy, a devotee of the pipe would simply take a tobacco leaf, crumble it in his hand, and place the shreds in the pipe bowl. He knew that if the leaf came from the base of the plant, the smoke would be strong and heavy; if the leaf came from the center portion of the stalk, the smoke would be fairly mild; and if the leaf had grown near the top of the plant, the smoke would be very light and rather tasteless.

Early American pipe smokers were also aware that the taste of the smoke varied according to the region where the tobacco plant was grown. They knew that their own Virginia leaves yielded a sweet, full-flavored smoke, that Persian tobacco gave a light, mild smoke, and that the acrid smoke of French tobacco was nearly unbearable.

Sometime during the nineteenth century, smokers discovered that by blending different tobaccos they could obtain various mixtures incorporating the best qualities of each type of tobacco. Any smoker could thus prepare his own mixture to suit his personal taste. Blended tobaccos became very popular, and the practice of blending persisted, so that the pipe mixture which you buy today may be a combination of as many as five or ten different tobaccos.

What makes the tobacco grown in Turkey different from that

grown from the same type of seed in the Carolinas? Many factors influence the quality of the smoke from a tobacco plant. Among them are the weather, altitude, soil, moisture, and rainfall of the

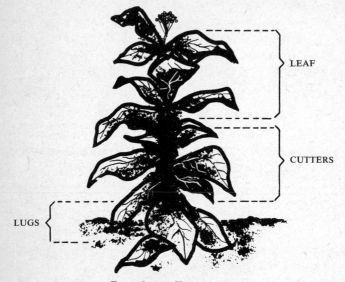

LEAF

CUTTERS

LUGS

FLUE-CURED TOBACCO PLANT

This figure shows the approximate stalk positions of the various grade groupings for flue-cured leaves. The most desirable leaves on the flue-cured plant are generally called "leaf" but may include many grades, depending upon the size, color and condition of the leaves themselves.

region. The cultivation is also of the greatest importance. Growers must choose the proper time to pick the leaves and perform the drying, curing, and other necessary processes. Just as wines derived from grapes grown in different vineyards may have different taste, tobacco from the same type of seed, but growing in adjacent plantations, may smoke very differently.

Moreover, during the curing process, organic changes take place in the leaf, similar to the action yeast has on dough. Much of the flavor of tobacco results from this fermentation process.

All these factors make tobacco blending somewhat of an art. Private blends have sometimes been handed down by tobacconists through several generations. As long as the tobaccos remain the same, so do the blends.

If you wish to make up your own blend, you should first become acquainted with the flavor and burning qualities of the various types of tobaccos. Then you can experiment with small amounts of selected tobaccos. When you have a satisfactory mixture, give the formula to your tobacconist and he will compound larger amounts for you upon request. Or you may find that a prepared blend suits your taste perfectly.

BURLEY TOBACCO

It is reasonably safe to say that burley tobaccos are smoked in more pipes than any other variety of tobacco. Burley is probably the best tobacco for a straight (unblended) smoke. The two types of burley, generally known as *Kentucky burley* and *white burley,* are both clean, cool-smoking tobaccos. White burley is very mild, with little flavor or aroma. Its neutral taste makes it ideal for mixing and reducing the strength of heavier-flavored tobaccos. Kentucky burley, while not quite as light-colored or smooth as the white variety, is still extremely mild when compared to some of the heavier tobaccos.

Both white burley and Kentucky burley are actually greenish-yellow or brownish-yellow in color, the "white" burley being somewhat lighter, hence its name. The two varieties of burley comprise the second largest tobacco crop in the United States, grown mostly in Tennessee, Kentucky, and southern Ohio.

Burley forms the basis of most tobacco blends, with many popular-priced mixtures containing as much as 75 per cent burley. Burley is also popular with manufacturers because it readily blends with other tobaccos. If you find your tobacco blend too harsh, too sweet, or generally too highly flavored, you can add as much as 50 per cent burley to your mixture. The result will be a milder blend which will yield a flavorful smoke.

VIRGINIA TOBACCO

Virginia tobacco has been cultivated in Virginia ever since colonist John Rolfe, husband of the Indian princess Pocahontas, first planted the seed there in 1612. Today the bulk of Virginia tobacco is grown in a much wider region, including Virginia, but also North Carolina, South Carolina, Florida, and Georgia. The best grade of Virginia tobacco, generally called *Virginia Bright,* is a light lemon-yellow color. Other grades of Virginia tobacco vary in color from light green to brown and dark tan, depending on the soil and processing.

Virginia, like burley, can be smoked straight or used as a base for blends. When smoked alone, it has a full, light-bodied flavor and a sweet taste resulting from its high natural sugar content. Actually, Virginia tobacco resembles burley except that it has more flavor and aroma and less oil, so that its smoke is very mild.

Virginia Bright is a flue-cured tobacco produced by controlled, even, smokeless heat being introduced into the curing barns by flues carrying hot air. The heat and moisture in the barn are carefully regulated during the entire curing process. Virginia Bright is usually cut fine for the pipe, and therefore smokes rather fast and hot.

Other types of Virginia tobacco include *Virginia Bright Pickings,* cured and cut somewhat differently from Bright. Several leaves are pressed together to form a "cake," and the cake then sliced to give a coarser cut. The result is a slower-burning tobacco, which yields a cooler, sweeter, more woody taste.

Virginia Plug Cut is similar to the Bright Pickings except that it has a much coarser cut. Producing a cool and very rich, mellow smoke, it is widely used in British blends.

Virginia Dark, grown in different kinds of soil, undergoes a fire-curing process by being exposed to an open fire. This tobacco has broad, dark-green leaves and is rarely used in pipe mixtures.

Virginia Sun-Cured, a regional variety grown almost exclusively near the city of Richmond, gets its name from an early practice of curing the leaves in the open sun. Today, most "sun-cured" tobaccos are actually cured in barns.

Pipe smokers owe it to themselves to become familiar with all types of Virginia tobacco, as well as the various cuts. Try each type, both as a straight smoke and as a blend. Too much Virginia in a mixture may make it bite, because the tobacco generally lacks essential oils. For this reason, plus the fact that it burns slowly, Virginia should not constitute more than 15 per cent of a mixture.

CAVENDISH TOBACCO

Practically all types of tobacco generally belong to one of two groups: those used as the "base" of a mixture, such as burley and Virginia, and those used for adding flavor, taste, and aroma to the blend, such as *Latakia, Perique,* and *Turkish.* But one tobacco, *Cavendish,* can be used both as a base and as a flavoring agent.

Cavendish is said to have received its name from Lord William Cavendish, the Duke of Newcastle, when he discovered this variety of tobacco around the year 1660.

Modern Cavendish differs from Virginia in that it is processed with sweetening agents such as maple sugar, sugar water, rum, or honey. This gives the tobacco a dark mahogany color and a very sweet flavor. Today, the word Cavendish often refers to other tobaccos, such as Virginia or *Maryland,* which have been similarly processed. The smoker may run across such varieties as *Virginia Cavendish, Cavendish Wine-Cured, Cavendish Dark Plug Cut, Honey Cavendish,* and *Shredded Cavendish.*

Cavendish can be smoked straight and many smokers prefer it that way. But it is often blended with other base tobaccos such as burleys and Virginias. If you are preparing your own blend, start by mixing equal amounts of Cavendish and burley. This will give you some idea of the use of Cavendish as a base. If you wish, you can keep adding Cavendish until it makes up as much as 90 per cent of the mixture.

To familiarize yourself with the use of Cavendish as a flavoring agent, first smoke a few pipefuls of plain white burley. Once you are familiar with this taste, add about 25 per cent Honey Cavendish to the blend. This will yield a mild smoke with very little aroma. For more flavor, you can add small amounts of Perique, Latakia, and other flavoring tobaccos. The variety of sweetening agents used to flavor Cavendish tobaccos makes it a never-ending source of interest to the pipe smoker who enjoys experimenting with new blends.

MARYLAND TOBACCO

Unlike other tobaccos, Maryland tobacco actually grows exclusively in the state from which it derives its name. It is cultivated in the southern part of Maryland, between the Potomac River and Chesapeake Bay. The gray-and-yellow sandy soil on which the tobacco is grown must be carefully prepared. After being cut, the tobacco leaves are cured in large barns by normal ventilation of the air, without artificial heat or fire.

The finished leaf, thin, dry, and holding fire very well, burns slowly. Smoked plain, it has a very subtle flavor; when blended, it adds little taste to the blend. For these reasons, it is often used in a mixture likely to burn too rapidly or with difficulty. Maryland can also be used to reduce a strong blend and give it a more neutral flavor.

The Maryland tobacco crop is small, and there are few varieties. The smoker should first try some plain Maryland, and then add to it one of the many flavoring tobaccos. As an experiment, some Maryland might be introduced into a mixture whose characteristics are already familiar to the smoker. Use Maryland sparsely when blending; the addition of as little as one part in sixteen will make a noticeable difference.

LATAKIA TOBACCO

One harvesting season about ninety years ago, an unusually large crop of tobacco was cut in northern Syria. Much of the tobacco remained unsold, and the ripe plants were hung from the roofs of the native houses, where the tobacco cured over the fires used to heat the dwellings. The fuel of the region which, some say, included camel dung, gave the tobacco a strong odor and color never experienced before.

It was found that this tobacco, when included in a blend, made an excellent flavoring agent. The new tobacco was discovered near the town of Lattaquie, from which it was to obtain its name, Latakia. Today, the tobacco is cured over the smoke of various aromatic herbs.

Unlike other tobaccos, the stem and ribs of the Latakia plant produce the best smoke. So, in its case, the entire plant—*including the flowers*—makes up the tobacco. The curing process instills it with a heavy, sweet flavor and a dark, oily appearance. As Latakia possesses a highly distinctive taste, only very small amounts are needed in a blend. One ounce in a pound is very noticeable, and it would be unwise to have more than 15 per cent Latakia in any mixture.

Found in most good smoking mixtures, Latakia is fine tobacco for adding spice, natural flavor, and aroma.

PERIQUE TOBACCO

Just about the time the American colonies were rising in revolt against the British King, an Acadian Frenchman named Pierre Chenet wandered into Louisiana and entered a region known as St. James Parish. There he observed the Choctaw and Chickasaw Indians processing tobacco in a hollow log by placing it under great pressure until the tobacco's natural juices were squeezed out. The Indians would then allow the leaves to soak and ferment in their own natural juices.

Chenet tested the resulting tobacco and found it to have a pronounced sweet and flavorful taste different from that of any other tobacco. He studied the process and improved on the Indians' methods. As the popularity of the new tobacco spread, it became known as "tabac de Perique," since Perique was Pierre's nickname.

Perique tobacco ranks as something special among tobacco plants. For some unknown reason, it grows only on a small triangle of land some fifty miles west of the city of New Orleans. All attempts to grow Perique seeds on other soils have failed. Since Perique has such unique flavor, 5 per cent in a blend is usually sufficient.

Perique adds flavor and aroma to mixtures, burns slowly, and reduces the bite of fast-burning tobaccos. Today, Perique curing methods are essentially the same as they were when discovered by Chenet; but the processes which yield this fine, flavorful tobacco have remained a mystery.

TURKISH TOBACCOS

Although the Western Hemisphere is the original home of the tobacco plant, many smokers feel that the world's choicest tobaccos come from parts of Turkey and other regions bordering the Black Sea. They are convinced that these tobaccos are unexcelled in aroma and flavor. The climate and soil of Turkey is in fact ideal for the growing of tobacco, and the plant has thrived there, gaining many desirable characteristics.

Turkish tobaccos grow not only in Turkey, but also in Macedonia, a part of Greece adjacent to Bulgaria, and other nearby countries. The name "Turkish" has carried over from the time when all these lands were under the hegemony of the Turks. There are many types of Turkish tobaccos, as well as different ways of growing, harvesting, and curing each type. Thus, innumerable variations in the finished tobacco have been the direct result. The following are some of the more common types of Turkish tobaccos:

Xanthi, is one of the finest Turkish varieties, often referred to as the "Queen of Tobaccos." It has a fresh, sweet, taste, a full body, and a very pronounced aroma. These qualities make it suitable as a flavoring element. It will give character to a mixture when added in small quantities. Xanthi production is relatively limited. Its cultivation is centered around the Greek town of Xanthi, from which it gets its name.

Djebel is very similar to Xanthi, since it is grown in the same geographical area. Djebel shares the same deliciously sweet flavor and grand aroma of Xanthi, but in smaller proportions. It burns and holds fire very well, has slightly less body than Xanthi, and therefore rates as a somewhat lighter tobacco.

Macedonian are tobaccos that grow in the Macedonian region of Greece. Macedonian tobaccos possess a mild, light taste, are very sweet, give off a pleasant aroma, and have excellent combustion qualities. Their mild yet fragrant character makes these tobaccos acceptable both as a base and as a flavoring agent.

Adrianople tobacco is cultivated in the peninsula which forms the European part of Turkey. Of medium quality, it produces a rather strong smoke and has a neutral taste. Most Adrianople tobacco is consumed in Europe and Asia. Very little of it ever appears in this country.

Smyrna is very rich tobacco grown along the west coast of Turkey. Famous for its pleasant aroma, some claim it to be the most aromatic of all tobaccos. Smyrna has a low rate of combustion but has a light, sweet taste which makes it a good addition to bland mixtures. Because of its heavy aroma, it should never be allowed to predominate in a blend.

Samsoun is a fine, pleasant tobacco cultivated in the east central part of Turkey, where the country's north shore touches the Black Sea. It is noted for its unusual, delicate, agreeable taste, which differs from that of any other tobacco. Samsoun will improve any blend and can perk up an otherwise mediocre mixture. This tobacco also enjoys excellent burning qualities.

Trabisond, a tobacco which grows near the Samsoun district, possesses an unusually strong, yet agreeable, taste. Trabisond is usually employed to increase the strength of a mixture.

Djubek is really a Russian tobacco, although the plant is the same as the Turkish Xanthi. It has a light, full-bodied taste and an especially strong, fine aroma. Many smokers consider it the finest oriental tobacco, and use it to add a touch of spice to their blends.

This is only a partial list of the many fine tobaccos available from the Near East. Turkish tobacco, as purchased at your tobacconist, may be any one of the types mentioned, or it may be a mixture of several different types. Seldom smoked straight, Turkish is used primarily as a flavoring agent since a little of it goes a long way. If you wish to do your own blending with Turkish tobaccos, start by adding one part Turkish to sixteen parts of burley or Virginia. You will be happily surprised by the new taste and aroma which even this small amount of Turkish tobacco will impart to the blend.

TOBACCO CUTS

The generally accepted methods of cutting tobacco are the result of trial-and-error experiments performed over many decades. All cuts are made either from single leaves, or from groups of pressed leaves. Any cutting of the single leaf is usually termed a "long" cut, while slicing the pressed leaves, or "cake," is referred to as a "plug" cut.

Single leaves can be broken up in a "chop cut," where the leaf is actually chopped into small pieces about one-quarter inch square. The leaf can also be "ribbon cut," in which case it is sliced into long, narrow strips. Chop-cut tobacco has fairly slow, cool-burning qualities. On the other hand, the thin, stringy structure of ribbon-cut tobacco, and the large air spaces between the shreds, make this type of cut burn fast.

The combustion of plug-cut tobacco is much slower than that of any chop cut or ribbon cut. Since several layers of leaves pressed tightly together with little space for air compose a section of plug cut, plug-cut tobacco takes a long time to ignite and even longer to burn. Accordingly, it tends to give a very cool smoke.

The smoker can vary the cuts of tobacco he employs so as to control the rate of burning. This in turn will affect the flavor of the tobacco, and will determine how many times a pipe has to be relighted. The types of cuts will also determine whether a mixture will hang together or not, and the manner in which it packs into the pipe bowl. In choosing tobacco cuts, experience is the best teacher.

The first step in mixing your own blend is to pay a visit to a leading tobacconist in any large city. He will usually carry a stock of straight, unblended tobaccos, such as burley, Cavendish, and Catakia. If the dealer does not have a particular tobacco or cut in stock, he probably will be glad to order it for you.

The base tobaccos are usually sold by the quarter-pound, half-pound, or pound, while the much stronger aromatic and flavoring tobaccos may be sold by the ounce. The dealer keeps the tobaccos in humidors and measures the correct amount by weight, using a balance scale.

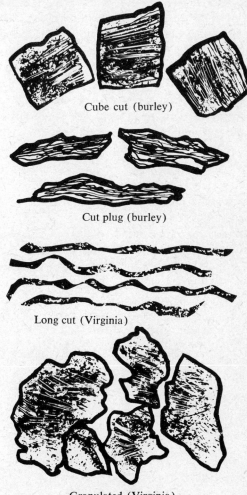

Cube cut (burley)

Cut plug (burley)

Long cut (Virginia)

Granulated (Virginia)

THE FOUR BASIC TOBACCO CUTS

In preparing your blend at home, you can measure by volume if you do not have a scale at hand. When you have prepared the desired amount of each tobacco, place the tobaccos in separate piles on a clean, level surface. Then mix the tobaccos together gently by using the open fingers of both hands as "forks." Keep mixing until all the tobaccos are evenly distributed through the blend; then store the mixture in your humidor.

Blending tobaccos to suit your particular taste, one of the great thrills of pipe-smoking, is both simple and difficult to achieve. It requires no special equipment and very little time. Yet it takes years of experience to make an intelligent appraisal of the qualities of various blends. Because of this, tobacco blending has remained an art, but it is an art which every pipe smoker can practice and enjoy.

Chapter 6

The Art and Science of Smoking

SMOKING A PIPE is such a common custom today that we tend to forget it is both an art and a science developed over four centuries.

It is an art in that a pipe is smoked for pleasure and pleasure only. It is a science in that the pipe bowl is a small furnace which, like any other furnace, must be properly fueled, fired, and cleaned in order to operate at its best. Unless these techniques are mastered, the smoker will find little joy in the use of his pipe.

Smoking in its earliest days was recognized as an art, and no man was considered a gentleman until he could smoke properly. Tutors and professors of smoking appeared on the scene, who, for a price, would teach the novice the fundamentals and mysteries of the art. The complete course began with a history of smoking, and included the technique of inhaling through the nose. The course ended when the student had mastered the skill of blowing smoke rings in the air.

The gentleman of fashion smoked at all times and at all places, in the theater as well as on the street. He carried in his pockets a complete smoking kit—a tobacco box, a pair of tongs for lighting his pipe with a burning coal, and a tobacco stopper for pressing the fired leaves firmly into his pipe bowl—all elaborately wrought of expensive materials. His pipe, however, was the same clay pipe smoked by common laborers and poor men in general.

Perhaps the most interesting time for the avid pipe smoker

came during the Victorian period. The nineteenth-century gentleman would have to retire to a special smoking-room, don a smoking-cap and jacket to protect his hair and clothes from the vile odor of tobacco, and puff away until interrupted by the ladies of the house. If there was no smoking-room, he would have to smoke secretly by his bedroom fireplace, surreptitiously blowing the smoke up the chimney so that no offensive odor would remain.

Fortunately, the modern smoker can enjoy a pipeful either in private or in public. Moreover, he'll always have a pleasant smoke if he is familiar with the art and science of smoking—breaking in, filling, lighting up, and cleaning the pipe.

Many a man who is attracted to pipe smoking gives up the practice after a few days because he finds little pleasure in his pipe. He finds that his tongue feels burned and is bitter-tasting, that the bowl becomes too hot to hold, or that the pipe will not stay lit. As a result, the would-be pipe smoker gives up in disgust, and the fraternity of pipe smokers has lost a friend. The fledgling smoker simply failed to realize that a pipe must be broken in and smoked properly before it will yield an enjoyable smoke.

To derive maximum pleasure and satisfaction from a pipe, the new smoker should follow a few important but simple steps:

1. The first step in breaking in a new pipe is to moisten the inside of the bowl with a little water applied with the finger. This will permit the carbon, formed by the burning of the tobacco, to cling to the walls of the briar and act as insulation against the heat of the first light-up. If the inside of the bowl has been pre-charred (or caked) by the pipe maker, however, this step should be eliminated.

2. Next, fill the bowl about one-half full of good tobacco. Fill the pipe gradually, tamping down each layer of tobacco firmly with the finger.

3. Now light the pipe evenly all around. Igniting the tobacco will cause it to rise up slightly in the bowl. Tamp down the tobacco with a metal tamper and relight evenly once again. If the bowl is packed correctly, you will have no trouble in keeping the tobac-

co lit.

4. It is extremely important to smoke the first few bowlfuls slowly. Indeed, it is always best to puff patiently away, no matter how well your pipe is broken in.

Form proper habits of filling and smoking your pipe from the moment you purchase it. Smoke the pipe slowly until the tobacco is burned down to the very bottom of the bowl. This not only prevents overheating, but also forms an even, protective cake on the walls of the bowl.

After smoking a few pipefuls, gently remove the ash or "dottle" from the bottom of the bowl with a pipe-smoker's "spoon." Be careful not to damage the thin, newly-formed cake. Now fill the bowl about three-quarter full and smoke it. Gradually increase the amount of tobacco until you have filled the bowl to the top. You'll find that your pipe will have gained that treasured possession—a regular, even cake from the bottom to the top of the bowl.

The cake is an accumulation of porous carbon, which fulfills two important functions: the carbon acts as a protective coating that helps prevent "burn-out," and is largely responsible for the sweetness of the smoke. It also blends into the smoke the flavor of genuine briar. This combined effect gives a pipe the mellow flavor which pipe-smokers always strive to achieve. The carbon cake should be developed slowly and evenly, and should form a uniformly thick lining on the pipe bowl. If your pipe is properly filled but still goes out occasionally while being smoked, it may be because you've packed the tobacco too tightly.

Once the protective cake is formed, don't remove it. However, after much smoking, even a well-broken pipe can develop an uneven cake. Too thick a cake may also become a menace to the life of your pipe. It can cause the pipe bowl to crack, because the carbon cake expands and contracts at a different rate than the briar. The different rate of expansion can create a tremendous pressure on the briar, especially if the pipe has a thick cake and is smoked rapidly, generating a great deal of heat.

The excess carbon must be removed in a simple but important operation called *reaming*. The ideal pipe reamer is one which fits the sides and bottom of the pipe bowl perfectly. Any good pipe shop will have a number of reamers that do this job effectively and are adjustable to fit any bowl.

The cake in the bowl should be reamed to the proper thickness (about one-sixteenth of an inch, or the breadth of a penny). Use the reamer sparingly, so that an even thickness of cake remains along the inner surface of the bowl.

The cutting edges of the reamer should be razor sharp. A dull reamer may force the smoker to chip and gouge the somewhat brittle cake. If the cake is inadvertently chipped down to the bowl wall, then the entire cake will have to be removed and a new cake slowly built up through smoking. To guard against this, avoid using knives and razor blades. Use the instrument specially designed for the job—a sharp, close-fitting pipe reamer. If a knife is used, go easy and be sure the job is smooth.

After smoking a new pipe for the first time, allow the ashes to remain in the bowl until cold so as not to disturb the newly-formed carbon cake. When the pipe has been well broken in, remove the ashes and "dottle" (the unsmoked tobacco at the bottom of the bowl) immediately after each smoking.

Some manufacturers coat the inside of the bowl with a prepared carbon cake mixture. This may or may not do the job. The vital ingredient in the cake mixture is usually sugar, which con-

Complete burnthrough, resulting from the pipe's owner having held the pipe in a downward position. This forced heat from burning tobacco to concentrate at a particular point of the bowl wall.

| The reamer should be an exact fit for the shape of the new pipe bowl. | The reamer is inserted into the bowl, to cut away the cake which has become too thick. | Following the reaming, only 1/16″ of carbon cake should remain. |

IMPROPER REAMING MAY DAMAGE THE PIPE BOWL

| Reamer inserted at incorrect angle. | Reamer inserted too close to one side. |

| Knife used instead of a properly-shaped reamer. | Reamer not same shape as the bowl. |

CORRECT AND INCORRECT PIPE REAMING

tains a great deal of carbon in its chemical structure. As the sugar burns, only the carbon remains. and the carbon absorbs the bitter green taste of tobacco bite. Similar to this method is the one of breaking in pipes with honey, which, consisting largely of sugar, has the same effect as sugar.

However, the newcomer may well prefer to break in his pipe himself, slowly, so as to give his pipe a chance to develop a natural cake lining in the pipe bowl. He will then enjoy the satisfaction of a mellow smoke, properly filtered through the cake lining and subtly blended with the flavor of briar.

To break in a new pipe so as to insure a pleasant smoke, just proceed as outlined:

1. **Moisten the inside** of the bowl with a little water applied by your finger tip.

2. **Fill the bowl** one-half full with good tobacco, evenly packed from the bottom of the bowl to the top.

3. **Light the tobacco evenly,** with a wooden match— tamp down the burning tobacco and relight evenly again.

4. **Smoke the pipe slowly,** so as to create an even cake. Smoke the pipe down to the bottom of the bowl, taking long draws and removing the pipe from your mouth between puffs.

5. **Allow the pipe to cool,** and remove the ashes by slapping the bowl on the palm of the hand. The bowl or bit may break if knocked against a hard object, such as a metal or glass ashtray.

Make sure that the inside of a new pipe is clean and smooth. Any irregularity or rough spot (fuzz) on the inner surface of the bowl could be the start of a charred spot. Once charring begins, it usually continues until the pipe burns out and consequently becomes worthless.

Why do pipes burn out? The answer is simple: heat. A briar pipe is not made of metal or asbestos; it's nothing more nor less than a wooden bowl and it will burn or char if it gets hot enough. To keep a pipe from burning out, care must be taken to prevent intense heat from reaching the bowl. This can be done by smoking slowly, and thus keeping the temperature of the tobacco down. Slow smoking will also allow a cake to form, which will protect the walls of the bowl from the excessive heat.

Well-made pipes are usually guaranteed against defects in manufacture and burn-outs which may result from such defects.

Good briarwood absorbs very little moisture during any one smoke, because the pores of the wood are very tight. Normally, after a few smokes, a pipe should be put away for a few days to allow this moisture to evaporate. If a new pipe is smoked too frequently, the moisture will have no chance to evaporate, and will accumulate in the bottom of the bowl, where the pipe is cooler. This yields a soggy pipe, sometimes called a pipe with a "wet heel."

The neophyte pipe smoker should also practice "smoking dry." This means that he should keep his saliva away from the bit. Any wet saliva entering the stem will increase the chances of having a foul-smelling pipe, with a bitter taste.

Excess moisture in the stem will also cause a gurgling sound every time you draw on the pipe. You can reduce the amount of saliva entering the pipe and maintain a dry bit by not holding the bit too far inside the mouth. Ordinarily, placing an object, such as the bit of a pipe, in the mouth will start a natural flow of saliva. If you swallow this excess saliva, instead of spitting it into the stem, the saliva flow will gradually decrease. This may take a little practice, but it will eliminate an annoying source of moisture.

FILLING THE PIPE

A man should fill his pipe the way an experienced woodsman builds a fire. Otherwise he is inviting trouble—in the form of a burned-out or burned-through pipe bowl. Before you even look in the direction of the tobacco jar, blow through the mouthpiece to make sure that the stem is clear. Then glance into the bowl to make sure that all the ashes and stale tobacco from your last smoke have been knocked out.

The simplest way to fill your pipe is to thrust it into the tobacco pouch and tamp in the tobacco with your fingers. The tobacco should be loose at the bottom of the bowl and firmly packed at the top. There is an old rule about filling pipes which expresses this principle very well: "Fill your pipe first with a child's hand, then a woman's, and finally a man's." After each pinch, insert your finger into the bowl and feel that the packing is of the correct firmness. When the bowl is full to the brim, use your thumb to press down and even out the surface tobacco.

A final press with the index finger will insure the proper packing so that the pipe will draw and smoke properly. An evenly packed and distributed surface will make it much easier to light the pipe.

If the pipe is packed too loosely, you will have to draw on it continuously just to keep it lit. If the pipe is too tightly packed, it may become too hot. If it is unevenly packed, the bowl will heat unevenly and may scorch the bowl or cause it to crack.

Check the draw of your pipe before lighting it. If it draws too freely, press in another pinch of tobacco. If it draws with difficulty, the pipe must be emptied and refilled. It may also be that a shred of tobacco is blocking the opening from the bowl into the stem. This is rarely the case with coarsely cut tobacco, but with the finer cuts some care must be taken in placing the first pinch.

Combustion in a pipe can be compared to that in a coal stove or furnace—the more draft, the hotter the fire. Therefore it becomes essential to smoke slowly. The more rapid the puffing, the more quickly the tobacco will burn and the hotter the smoke. Pause between each puff, puff gently, and you will enjoy a cooler smoke.

LIGHTING UP

There is no simpler way for two strangers to strike up a conversation than for one to ask the other for a match. A match is used very matter-of-factly by most of us. We strike it, light our pipe, blow it out, and discard it. But matches were not always readily available. The early colonists in America had but two methods of lighting a fire: one, with flint and steel, and the other by rubbing firesticks together, a slow but reliable way. When an early settler, John Brereton, visted in 1605 what is now Rhode Island, he wrote:

"They strike fire in this manner: every man carryeth about him a purse of sewed leather, a Minerall stone (copper) and with a flat Emeric stone (flint) tied fast to the end of a little sticke, gently he striketh upon the Minerall stone and within a stroke or two, a sparke falleth upon a piece of Touchwood and with the least sparke he maketh fire presently."

More than two centuries later, Charles Dickens, in describing the same slow process, wrote, "On a damp day, with luck, one might get a light in half an hour."

Many types of matches were invented in the nineteenth century to supply a world dissatisfied with the stubbornness of the tinder-box. One very useful type was the "Drunkard's Match," created by the Diamond Match Company in 1882. The splint of the match was treated so that it would not burn beyond its midpoint. In this way a tipsy smoker could avoid burnt fingers.

One of the earliest matches, the "Lucifer Match," was three inches long, and tipped with antimony, sulphide, gum and starch. Lucifer matches were struck by being drawn through a pleat of sandpaper, and they ignited with a series of small explosions and a shower of sparks. These matches smelled so that one manufacturer printed this warning on his boxes:

"If possible, avoid inhaling the gas that escapes from the combustion of the black composition."

This warning still applies today to the modern pipe smoker. Let the tip of the match burn off before touching the flame to the tobacco in your pipe; otherwise, you may inhale a mouthful of choking sulphur and phosphorous fumes, and ruin your smoke.

Always use matches when lighting a pipe—preferably long wooden kitchen matches, not paper matches. Several good mechanical lighters are on the market today, They provide a steady, sizeable flame that lights the tobacco evenly. Of course, if you happen to be sitting near a warm hearth with a fire in the grate, simply pick up a glowing coal to light your pipe. This is probably the most satisfying way of lighting up. Leave the ember on the surface of the tobacco until the pipe is properly lit. If you prefer, keep the ember in the bowl until the pipe is smoked out—

it will add its own flavor to that of the tobacco.

When lighting the pipe, keep the bowl upright; place the heat of the match on the tobacco; and draw strongly. The flow of air will draw the flame downward into the bowl and ignite the tobacco. Don't turn the pipe to one side or place it upside down. This will result only in unevenly lit tobacco and burnt briar. By drawing the flame into the bowl, you can see exactly which areas need lighting. Circle the lighted match over the tobacco in the bowl so that the entire surface becomes aglow; then the tobacco will burn evenly and smoothly down the bowl as your smoke progresses.

How does a pipe burn tobacco? When a pipe is lit, the heat of the flame causes the organic compounds in the tobacco to react with the oxygen in the air; the result of this reaction is primarily water vapor, carbon dioxide, and a carbon residue. But the pipe bowl is not a perfect combustion chamber, and not all of the tobacco becomes reduced to those three substances. As the heat flows through the bowl, it produces a number of other effects. First, the heat dries out the tobacco directly below the burning zone. Second, the heat vaporizes oils out of the tobacco in the burning zone. Third, the non-volatile carbonaceous material is burned to ash.

When the pipe is lit, some moisture, oil vapor, and some smoke particles from the hot zone condense on the surface of the cooler tobacco below, on the cooler bowl, and in the stem. As the hot zone burns on down inside the bowl, part of this condensed material is revaporized and part is burned off. Some collects at the very bottom of the bowl and forms a "dottle"; this should be removed after each smoke so that the pipe can dry out thoroughly. This will insure the sweetness of the next smoke.

Several factors make the difference between a cool and a hot smoke. The faster you smoke, the hotter the pipe and its contents become. This, it must be repeated, makes it obligatory to smoke slowly. A second factor is the importance of having a dry pipe. A pipe should "rest" between smokes to allow the circulation of air to carry off any moisture collected in the bottom of the bowl.

THE ART AND SCIENCE
OF SMOKING

CLEANING THE PIPE

A pipe smoker who pays strict attenton to the cleaning of his pipe will get a more enjoyable smoke every time. This ritual is one of the many pleasant activities that goes with pipe smoking, but should be carried out regularly and carefully.

Be very cautious when removing the stem from the bowl for a cleaning. In a new pipe the fit is often so tight that the stem or wood will crack if care is not taken. Always remove the stem by twisting it, never by pulling. Don't grasp the stem by its tip; instead, get a firm grip near the point where the stem enters the shank of the bowl. Never remove the stem while the pipe is still warm.

In general, the pipe should be cleaned after every smoke by running a pipe cleaner through the stem and removing any ash or tobacco residue in the bowl. It should then be placed in a pipe rack with the stem pointing up and the bowl down. This will allow air to circulate through both stem and bowl.

After several smokes, a more thorough cleaning job is in order. Remove the stem (as previously described) and run a pipe cleaner through it. Now double up another pipe cleaner and swab out the shank boring. If your pipe has a metal filter, wipe off any moisture with a piece of tissue paper. Be lavish in the use of pipe cleaners—it pays dividends in sweeter, cleaner smoking.

When the carbon cake has become thicker than one-sixteenth of an inch, it should be trimmed down by the use of a special reamer found in any good pipe shop, and whose use was detailed earlier in this chapter. If the cake is allowed to become too thick, the difference in rate of expansion between the briar and the cake could result in a cracked bowl.

By observing the techniques described in this chapter, you may be sure that pipe smoking will be a happy and rewarding experience. That this is in fact the purpose of pipe smoking was recognized by some of the earliest pipe smokers — African natives living along the Congo River. They tell the tale about the first smoker in their tribe. As the story goes, this imaginative fellow returned from a journey, bringing back with him the secrets of pipe smoking. He introduced his fellow-tribesmen to the virtues of the habit by describing its mellowing effect on his personality. He said that during his travels he had taken offense at someone and harbored thoughts of murder. But first he sat down and smoked a pipe of tobacco. He then reflected that a thrashing would be a more suitable vengeance than killing. After smoking a second pipe, he concluded that a scolding would be more proper than physical punishment. Finishing a third pipe, he found it in his heart to forgive the man and forget the whole incident.

And so it should be with all pipe smokers.

PATENT OFFICE MONSTROSITY

Chapter 7

How Briar Pipes Are Made

IT IS NO EASY TASK to transform a rough piece of natural briar into a fine pipe—a pipe that that will smoke well and remain an object of lasting beauty. Skilled craftsmen plus the best modern machinery are required to create today's high-quality pipe.

Before the development of the power-turning lathe, all pipes were made by hand. Pipe making was a carver's art, passed on for generations from father to son. Early briar pipes were ornately carved and as abundantly decorated as their forerunners, the clays and the meerschaums. Hand-carved pipes are still available today from most pipe manufacturers. These pipes come in various shapes and designs, depicting the heads of famous people, or animals, or many kinds of objects. But since the end of the First World War, the trend has been away from ornamented hand-carved designs.

Although the pipe-carving art is still practiced, most of today's pipe smokers prefer the perfectly turned bowl, sleek finish, and scientific design of pipes made with power machinery. This does not mean that automatic machines turn out modern quality pipes by the million. On the contrary, it is highly unlikely that quality pipe manufacture will ever be automated.

It takes as many as eighty individual operations to transform a briar block into a finished pipe. Skilled craftsmen, with years of experience and time-tested judgment, control each of these operations. The machines they use merely provide the power and precision to produce a perfect pipe — something no hand craftsmen could ever hope to achieve.

CUTTING THE BURL

The creation of a briar pipe begins not in the factory but in the region where the briar grows. When a digger has unearthed a briar burl, he chops away the inferior portions; then he brings the burl to a sawmill.

The men who process the briar first must dry up all the moisture within the burls. They place the freshly cut briar in long, shallow trenches and cover it with damp earth and straw. This permits the briar to mellow slowly without drying out too quickly. It is said that the best briar burls are those from plants which remain in the ground for several years. This presumably allows the moisture to dry out completely.

Skilled workers then use high-speed circular saws to slice each burl into several pieces. After each slice is cut away, it is examined for cracks, flaws, or inferior wood. Each slice is then segmented into a number of more or less perfect briar blocks, roughly pipe-shaped, and called *ebauchons*. A large prime burl will yield up to fifty briar blocks. From each block, a single pipe will be made.

Most briar blocks from which pipes are eventually carved are about three inches in length, and a burl must be at least this diameter to be of any use. Young burls, however, are so small that almost an entire burl is required to make a pipe. Such a small burl does not make a good pipe because the entire burl must be used, including the poorer sections.

Not all parts of the burl are of the best quality. The section where the soft, pulpy briar trunk passes through the burl is considered inferior. In fact, the trunk section within the burl differs only slightly from ordinary lumber. Thus, the choicest briar blocks are those cut from the sides of the burl, where the wood is hard and tightly grained. For this reason, some quality pipe manufacturers buy entire burls from the growers and cut the burl in their own workshops. Such procedure insures that the

Standard shape for a
briar block

Partly-formed briar pipe shaped
by machine, so as to simplify
hand carving

manufacturer's best pipes will be made from only the choicest wood.

It takes at least forty years for a burl to grow to a size large enough so that pipes carved from it do not incorporate the poorer wood of the trunk. Therefore, the choicest burls are the venerable ones (often more than one hundred years old), possessing the right size and sturdiness. Four-year-old, or even twelve-year-old, briar burls usually yield inferior pipes. A pipe made of briar cut from inside the burl (not including the trunk) will usually possess superb grain and be free from flaws.

CURING THE BRIAR BLOCKS

Briar is wood and, like all wood when freshly cut, contains moisture in the form of sap. Ordinary green wood, such as a pine board, may be cured simply by allowing its sap to dry. When pine lumber is made into a table or chair, it never experiences intense heat. As a result, it gives satisfactory performance. But a piece of briar made into a pipe becomes, in fact, a small furnace. As a result, it must be treated differently.

If the sap were allowed to remain in the briar, it would melt when subjected to heat, and would soon be forced to the surface of the bowl, where it would appear as a sticky mess. Some of the sap would also be consumed along with the tobacco inside the bowl, and the smoker would experience a bitter, unpleasant taste.

The removal of the natural sap also allows the wood to "breathe." Pipes made from the best wood correctly cured will give a sweet smoke and increasing satisfaction over the years.

To remove the tar and resins which have hardened with the briar blocks, the briar is boiled from twenty-four to forty-eight hours, or longer. At the end of that time, the tars and resins have been replaced with water, and the water is then allowed to evaporate. The drying must be done slowly, otherwise the blocks will split and become useless.

The blocks are dried for a minimum of three months, and up to three years in certain cases. For this entire period they are kept in a moisture-free room at normal temperature, protected from the weather, but not subject to artificial heat. The blocks are then placed in special drying rooms, and air is circulated over the entire surface of each block. Over a period of several weeks, workers slowly raise the temperature in these rooms. The operation is complete when the wood is bone dry.

The blocks are then graded and bundled into burlap bags for shipment, each bag containing from sixty to eighty-five dozen blocks.

When the dried blocks reach the pipe factory, they must pass through the hands of skilled inspectors, who grade the blocks according to size and possible flaws. Some surface defects may extend deeply into the block; other buried flaws may not be noticeable until after the block is cut. Men who have worked with briar for many years usually do the inspecting. They save the manufacturer the expense of shaping a pipe that will later have to be discarded.

SHAPING THE BOWL

The first actual shaping operation performed on the block is that of fashioning the bowl. Specially adapted woodworking lathes, equipped with extremely hard metal cutters not easily dulled by tough briarwood, are used for this job. Nevertheless, the briar is so hard that these cutters must frequently be sharpened.

The block, held firmly in a vise, is pushed slowly onto a high-speed revolving bit—which looks somewhat like an old-fashioned lemon squeezer, with two wing blades attached. The revolving bit bores the inside of the bowl and shapes the outside at the same time, down to the level of the shank. This operation demands the utmost skill. The bowl must be centered and bored to the precise, correct depth. The shape of the bowl and the thickness of its wall at various points must be scientifically proportioned according to the weight and design of the pipe.

SHAPING THE PIPE

After the upper part of the bowl has been bored and shaped, the remainder of the pipe, including the shank, is accurately shaped on a "frazing" machine. This device holds a metal model of the particular pipe design to be copied. A cam moves along the metal model and forces a cutting wheel to follow the shape of the model as it cuts through the briar block. The frazing machine resembles, in principle, the machine a locksmith uses in making copies of keys.

The metal model on the frazing machine determines the style and size of the finished pipe. Practically all pipe manufacturers follow the generally accepted styles, such as billiard, pear, apple, Dublin, and bulldog. However, each pipe manufacturer includes small variations to make his pipe shape distinctive.

As the pipe takes shape on the frazing machine, a skilled craftsman with a sharp eye watches for defects, which appear suddenly as the surface of the wood is cut away. If the flaw is shallow, it may be removed in future finishing steps. If it is deep, the pipe will have to be scrapped. A pipe maker proud of his workmanship never stamps his name on an imperfect pipe.

BORING THE SHANK

After the shank and bowl have been cut to shape, the next step is to bore a hole in the shank large enough to take the tenon—the part of the stem that fits into the shank—one of the most delicate and important operations in making the pipe. If the direction of the cut is not true, the walls of the shank will lack uniform thickness, and the pipe will be out of balance. Also, the hole may fail to pierce the bowl at its exact bottom point. Shank-drilling is a precise task that only the most skilled pipe makers can perform.

A hand-operated, electrically powered drill is used to bore an air chamber in the center of the shank, up to a depth of about one inch. The next step is more difficult. Every piece of briar has hard and soft spots, straight grain and twisted grain, the result of the briar plant's struggle during its growth. Briar is not a homogeneous material, like plastic or metal. It takes a sensitive hand to detect when the drill is penetrating the shank too rapidly, due to a soft spot, or when it is boring too slowly, due to a hard spot or particle of sand embedded in the briar. A twist in the grain direction might deflect the drill, causing it to bore off-center.

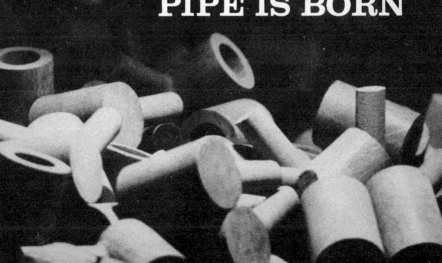

a
PIPE IS BORN

The briar blocks from which pipes will be shaped must first be air-dried and cured under controlled heat for several months (*center, top*). Blocks are graded as to shape and size (*center, bottom*). The bowl is then partially turned by high-speed rotating cutters (*left; right, top*). The cutting tool turns the inside and outside of the bowl simultaneously. The turned block is clamped in a frazing machine which shapes the shank and lower half of bowl (*right, bottom*). Block is forced against frazing cutters to duplicate a pre-selected pipe shape.

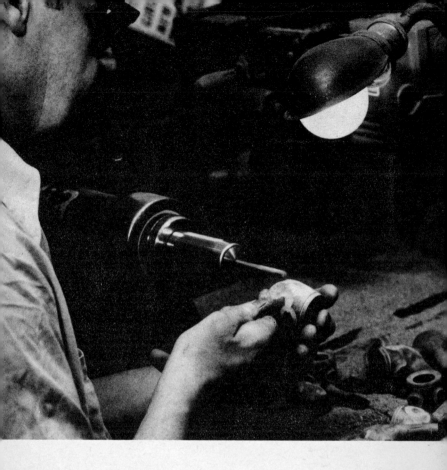

Drilling the shank of the briar bowl is a delicate operation requiring skilled hands. The tenon hole is first drilled (*left, top*) to accomodate the tenon of the stem. The air hole is then drilled through the shank into the bowl (*left, bottom*). The tenon hole is also reamed to thousandth-of-an-inch tolerance to insure a tight-fitting stem, which is then fitted (*left, bottom*). Sanding wheels of various grades of sandpaper then give a smooth finish (*right, bottom*). The bowl surfaces of selected pipes are then hand-carved with high-speed cutters (*right, top*).

97

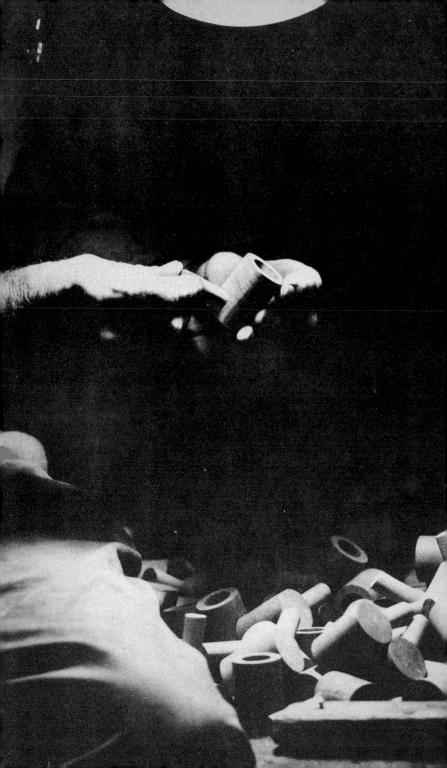

After sanding, the pipes must pass a rigorous inspection (*left*). Pipes with undesirable flaws, cracks, or irregularities are rejected. The pipes are stained to bring out the full grain and color of the briar (*right, top*). They may then be polished with a special preparation. A final buffing operation (*right, bottom*) imparts a lustrous sheen to the finished pipe. The inside of the bowl is caked with a charcoal mixture.

A specially designed machine routs a tiny groove in the stem (*left*), into which the pipe-maker's emblem will be inserted. The final inspection of the finished pipes is made by Carl Weber (*right*). He evaluates the pipes according to the beauty of their grain, the absence of flaws, the true bore of the air hole, and the quality of the finish. In determining the quality of each pipe, Carl Weber draws on more than fifty years of experience in pipe manufacture.

Photos Taken in the Weber Pipe Factory

PIPE STEMS

After the shank has been drilled, the pipe stem is fitted to the pipe itself. The size of the tenon and the hole in the shank must match to within a small fraction of an inch in order to insure a snug fit. If the tenon turns out to be too small, or the hole in the shank too big, the stem will be loose and pull out easily. If the fit is too tight, on the other hand, the pipe smoker is likely to break the shank or stem when trying to remove the latter for cleaning.

Any hard, durable, and tasteless material is suitable for making a pipe stem or bit. An ideal inexpensive material commonly used in most modern pipes is vulcanite, another name for hard rubber. Amber, both rare and expensive, is also used on occasion. Some manufacturers use transparent or colored plastic stems, but these are often very brittle and hard on the teeth. On the other hand, soft bits are prone to lose their shape, especially if the pipe is allowed to become warm. Stems of wood or ivory and other exotic materials have never stood up to the demands of pipe smoking, and are seen only rarely nowadays.

Vulcanite may be purchased by the manufacturer in pre-bored, long, black cylinders. The manufacturer then cuts it to the desired length, and shapes it with grinding wheels. Fine abrasives are used so that the bit will take on its own distinctive, lustrous, velvety polish. Unusual stem shapes are cut from large vulcanite blocks.

Curved stems are made by softening the bits with heat and bending the tubing to the desired shape. When the bit cools, its curve is permanently set.

More often, hard rubber bits are formed in compression or injection molds. In compression molding, vulcanite powder is compressed, through heat, into a half-stem shape. Two halves are then joined together with heat, and the joining mark ground off. In injection molding, molten rubber is forced under pressure into a die. The die is then cooled by immersing it in water, after which it is opened to yield a perfectly shaped pipe stem.

Many manufacturers purchase their pipe stems ready-made, so that the stems must only be custom-fitted to the pipes and finished. All the final sanding and polishing operations are performed with the stem firmly in the pipe. This insures that the pipe and stem will match perfectly. That is why you cannot take two similar pipes and transpose the stems. For the stems will rarely, if ever, match.

Now a word about amber. Beautiful, golden-yellow amber consists of petrified resin, solidified into a hard, resilient substance over hundreds of years. Found along the cost of the Baltic Sea, it is mined like any other precious or semi-precious stone. Then it is divided into rectangular cakes from which craftsmen fashion the beautiful pipe stems. Unfortunately, amber is highly flammable. It may burst into flame during the manufacturing operations, or even while the smoker is puffing on it. As mentioned earlier, amber is so expensive that it is rarely seen outside of pipe collections or on top quality meerschaum pipes.

FINISHING THE PIPE

Even after the craftsman has rough-shaped the pipe on the frazing machine and fitted it with a stem, many operations are still required before the pipe is ready to be smoked. It must be hand-sanded down to a very smooth, even finish through the use of progressively finer grades of sandpaper, spread over high-speed wheels that conform to the shape of the pipe. As many as fifteen grades of sandpaper may be employed in polishing.

A final sanding with a very fine emery cloth leaves the bowl and shank as smooth and clean as a spotless piece of glass. The sanding proceeds under the constant vigilance of experienced workers whose alert eyes detect the most minute flaws. If these craftsmen suspect that a flaw penetrates deeply within the wood, the pipe is discarded. The pipe stem also receives its share of sanding and a final finishing with a fine emery cloth.

Ordinary stone found buried deep in briar block shows how rocky soil is where briar grows.

After the pipe gets its final dress, the pipe maker may pass it on to an expert carver. A pipe may often be chosen for carving if it has minor surface defects, *but this is not necessarily so*. The carving may eliminate surface blemishes which would have little or no effect on the smoking qualities of the pipe. The expert pipe carver knows how to give any pipe a new face, depending on its size, shape, and quality. The carving expert may well produce a more beautiful pipe—lighter, easier on the teeth, and one that cools off faster due to the increased surface area produced by the indentations on the carved bowl.

Minor surface imperfections, which would not impair the smoking quality of the pipe, are filled so that the finished pipe will possess a smooth, even surface.

The pipe now undergoes inspection for grain and quality. It it is a top-grade pipe with outstanding grain, it may receive only a coat of oil or hard carnauba wax before the final buffing and polishing. As an alternative, the beauty of the briar grain may be brought out by staining. Light, delicate colors result in finishes such as russet oak, virgin, or walnut. Bowls with less distinctive grain patterns show up beautifully if stained in the darker cherry or plum colors.

After staining, some pipes may be lacquered or varnished; others may just be oiled or waxed. Buffing follows on all types of pipes, both stained and virgin briars. The buffing wheels bring out grain pattern, remove excess stain, and help the color penetrate into the briar.

Pipes not intended to receive a smooth finish may be sandblasted, giving a finish variously called "thorn," "rustic," "relief," or "shell." The jet of sand cuts away the softer parts of the grain, leaving the hard portions standing out like the shell of a walnut. Another type of processing involves boiling the briar bowls in oil for several days. This gives them a dark color without the use of any stain or varnish that might clog the pores of the wood.

After finishing, the pipe is ready for a final examination—an examination that largely determines the price. The inspector checks the cleanliness of the bowl, the trueness of the hole in both bowl and shank, the snug fit of the stem, the quality of the waxing and staining processes, the beauty of the grain, and the pipe's overall balance and appearance. This inspection determines the ultimate selling price of the pipe.

Pipe making will remain an art as long as nature supplies the briar for craftsmen to shape.

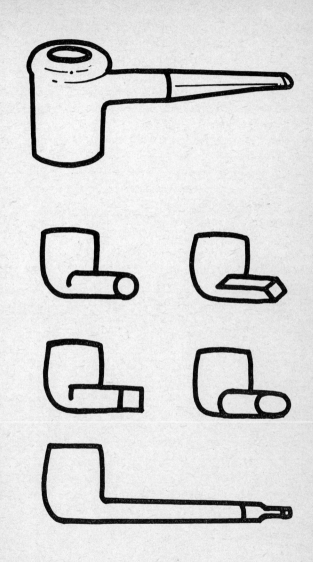

Chapter 8

Pipe Accessories

THE SERIOUS PIPE SMOKER will soon discover that a number of accessories are essential for the maintenance of his pipe and tobacco. Of course, it *is* possible to smoke a pipe without any additional equipment; but it seems foolish to spend ten dollars for a fine pipe, take the time and effort to break in the pipe properly, and then ruin the pipe by improper maintenance and poor smoking practices.

PIPE CLEANERS

Pipe cleaners, either with stiff bristles or soft fluffy threads set in wire, are the smoker's constant aids. They cost very little and should be used generously to clean both the pipe stem and shank, preferably after every smoke. Stiff wire or plastic cleaners can be used first to scour the air passages and remove any gummy deposits. These should be followed by softer cleaners which will absorb all the oily and liquid residues.

Cleaners are available in a variety of lengths and coarseness. The longer the tufts on the soft cleaners, the better cleaning job they will do.

Moisten coarse-brush pipe cleaners with pipe-cleaner liquid (available at good pipe shops) before use. In that way they will more readily dissolve any gummy impurities.

PIPE SWEETENERS

Keep a small bottle of pipe-cleaner fluid always at hand for pipe cleaning. This liquid dissolves the tars and oils produced by·the burning tobacco and sweetens the pipe.

If a commercial pipe sweetener is used, make sure it does not contain acetone or acids, as they are not beneficial to the briar. You can make your own sweetener, if you wish, by mixing pure grain alcohol with oil of wintergreen or oil of cloves. The result is a pleasant and efficient pipe-cleaning liquid and sweetener.

HUMIDORS

If you prefer to buy a few ounces of tobacco at a time, and then proceed to smoke it right then and there, you have no need for a humidor. However, if you prefer to save money by buying tobacco in larger quantities, or if you prefer to have your own blend made up by your tobacconist, you will need a suitable container in which to preserve the tobacco against the effects of time and weather.

The tobacco jar, or humidor, can be made of wood, ceramic, glass, or any other chemically neutral material.

Most important, the humidor should be airtight, so as to prevent the tobacco from losing too much moisture. As tobacco readily absorbs odors, never leave the tobacco jar open longer than necessary. Keep a piece of porous clay, plaster of Paris, or soapstone within the humidor at all times to replace the moisture inevitably lost by evaporation. This humidifying material, or humectant, should be moistened with water at regular intervals. Fasten it inside the lid of the jar, or some other spot where it will not come into actual contact with the tobacco.

TOBACCO POUCHES

Any small, flexible, and relatively airtight container that fits easily in your pocket can be used as a pouch. However, don't count on your pouch to keep tobacco moist for as long a time as will your humidor.

Most pouches are not completely airtight. In choosing a pouch, avoid those with fabric or ordinary rubber liners. These materials will crack within a few months. They will absorb and react with oils in the tobacco and add an unpleasant odor to your smoke.

THREE POPULAR TOBACCO POUCHES

Folding roll-up pouch

Zipper pouch

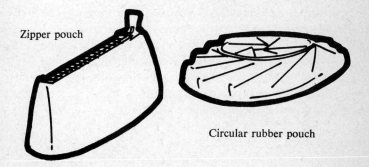

Circular rubber pouch

All-plastic pouches, or pouches with latex rubber linings, are preferable. Leather pouches are sometimes used too, and, when suitably lined, keep tobacco fresh.

Zipper pouches are convenient, and are easy to use. Another kind of pouch, made of plastic or some other non-porous material, is almost completely airtight when folded. The folding roll-up pouch also holds a great deal of tobacco and provides ample room to accommodate the pipe bowl and a couple of fingers as well, all which makes pipe-filling easy.

If you intend to carry a filled pouch for some time without replenishing it, enclose a small humidifying unit to keep the tobacco moist. This unit generally consists of a small perforated metal box filled with absorbent clay or some other humectant. A good pouch can be relied on to provide moist tobacco even when the smoker is far from his favorite humidor.

PIPE RACKS

A pipe collection is an investment deserving adequate protection. Any device that holds the pipe in a vertical position, with the bowl down, can serve as a pipe rack. It can be a simple home-made version, or, if you prefer, you may choose from a wide selection of pipe racks offered by commercial manufacturers. The vertical position of the pipe allows moisture in the stem and shank to run down into the bowl, where it will evaporate or be consumed in the next smoke.

If you possess a large pipe collection, you may wish to keep your most treasured pieces in individual cases, so as to prevent accidental breakage. This precaution is an especially good idea with meerschaum pipes. If you keep your pipe in a separate case, clean and dry it very thoroughly before storing it away. Since the pipe will not be in vertical position, any trapped moisture will remain in the stem and shank.

ASH TRAYS

A pipe smoker's ash tray should differ from those ordinarily used for cigars or cigarettes in two major respects: it should be quite large in order to prevent ashes and unburned tobacco from settling on furniture, and it should have a soft rubber or cork knocker against which the bowl can be struck without fear of breaking the pipe.

WIND CAPS

If you expect to smoke your pipe out-of-doors in windy weather, you must provide your pipe with a wind cap. The wind cap performs three important functions: (1) it prevents the wind from

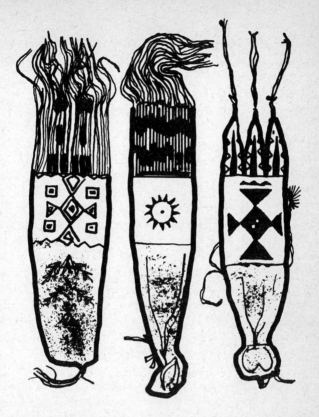

Three highly decorated tobacco pouches made and used by American Indians.

blowing the burning tobacco out of the bowl and perhaps setting a fire; (2) it keeps the tobacco from burning too rapidly and thus maintains a cool smoke; (3) by slowing down combustion, it also keeps the pipe bowl from charring and cracking.

Wind caps are available to fit any style or size of pipe. This inexpensive little device that snaps into place inside the top of the bowl is worth many times its price.

PIPE TOOLS

Since the pipe bowl must be reamed out occasionally, a reamer rates as an absolute necessity. If the smoker has a reamer which fits his pipe exactly, so much the better. However, if he has a large pipe collection, he need not have a different reamer for each pipe. There are a number of adjustable reamers on the market whose cutting edges can be adjusted to fit any pipe bowl. They also position themselves during the reaming process so as to leave an even cake within the bowl. The reamer should never be too sharp, for it might then crack or gouge both the cake and the bowl itself.

SMOKER'S COMPANION

Another popular pipe tool is the "smoker's companion"— a metal device that combines a pick, a tamper and a spoon in a single instrument. The tamper can be used to pack down the tobacco during smoking; the pick can be used to dislodge slugs from the air passages; and the spoon helps remove tobacco ash from the bowl. This is a small, handy gadget which fits easily into any pocket.

OTHER PIPE-SMOKING ACCESSORIES

Pipe-smoking perfectionists have devised a number of other accessories which you may find will add pleasure to your smoking. Among these are meerschaum or metal buttons, placed in the bottom of the pipe bowl in order to prevent the juices in the heel from contaminating the burning tobacco.

Atomizers are also sometimes used to moisten the tobacco uniformly. For more elaborate pipe-cleaning, retorts can be employed to force a pipe-cleaning liquid through the stem and bowl.

Chapter 9

The Pipe as a Hobby

COLLECTING PIPES is an old and established pastime. Men were collecting pipes when postage stamps had not as yet been invented. Indeed, the requirements of pipe collecting are among the simplest of any hobby: any smoker can be said to have a pipe collection if he has more than one pipe.

A pipe collection need not be large, nor must it consist only of expensive pipes. While, admittedly, a hand-carved meerschaum may cost hundreds of dollars, a plain, three-dollar briar possessing special personal meaning to the smoker certainly deserves equal respect as part of his collection.

Collecting pipes differs from collecting stamps, coins, or similar objects in that the pipes can always be used. The hobbyist's pipes serve a double purpose, since they are both items of special interest and instruments capable of providing an enjoyable smoke.

Most interested pipe smokers become collectors sooner or later. This does not mean they assemble a hundred or more pipes; but every smoker eventually learns that he should have at least four or five pipes and smoke them alternately. Soon the smoker finds himself with eight, ten, or fifteen pipes, so that he has quite naturally and progressively become a collector on a small scale.

Not all pipes which might grace a collection can be smoked. Many of them are too old and too fragile to withstand regular smoking. Yet the beauty and history of such pipes might give them great value. Every pipe collector usually separates his pipes into two classifications: those which can be regularly smoked, and those which should remain safely in their cases or behind glass.

The neophyte collector should learn all he can about pipes, both modern and historical. Libraries will have some books on the subject, but generally pipe literature is rather scarce. Pipe catalogues supplied by manufacturers often contain valuable information.

Your favorite pipe shop might also be helpful, or a local pipe club if one exists in your community. In most large cities there are museums and historical societies, many of which have pipe collections or pipe exhibits on display. You will want to know about different types of briar, stem sizes, shapes, and other details of pipe lore worth studying.

It is a good idea to add only good-quality pipes to your collection. Careful selection and an appreciation of quality will start you off on the road to becoming a pipe connoisseur. There is no reason to limit yourself to briar pipes; pipes of meerschaum, clay, various woods, and even corncobs and water pipes will liven up your collection.

The older carved meerschaum pipes are both beautiful and expensive. The meerschaums of forty or fifty years ago can still be found at reasonable prices. Also available are novelty pipes made of such materials as stone, glass, or ceramic. You may often pick them up as souvenirs of excursions or holidays. Your assemblage of pipes can even expand to include bizzare pipes from the Orient and Africa, aboriginal native pipes, and ancient pre-Columbian pipes, if you can get your hands on them before a museum does.

Where can these pipes be obtained? In facing this problem, the true collector must show both ingenuity and imagination. The search may begin by first visiting his local pipe shop, then hunting through local curio and antique shops. There you will probably find the most common and most plentiful types, such as the Central European porcelain pipes popular a century ago. They usually have a porcelain bowl, a cherry-wood stem, and a bone or horn bit. The bowl may be painted and the pipe decorated with cords and tassels. Such pipes are not expensive, and a few of them will add color and variety to any collection.

You may turn up a pipe which you suspect is quite old. Try to trace its history as far back as you can. It may have some association with a historical figure, which might make it valuable. How much would you give for Mark Twain's corncob, or for a church-warden smoked by Alexander Hamilton?

The collector's fun really begins when he takes an afternoon off to go sleuthing around pipe shops and antique dealers, searching for the rare and treasured pipe which, surprisingly, he will often find.

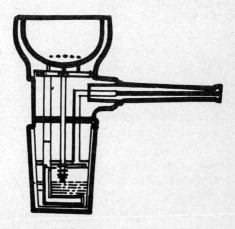

The search for the "better pipe" goes on and on. Here is but one extremely complicated pipe design on file at the U.S. Patent Office.

But the pipe hobbyist should by no means limit himself to ancient or historical pipes. If you see a pipe you particularly like in a tobacconist's window, add it to your collection. A collection of fine modern pipes can be especially rewarding because all the pipes in it can be smoked.

EVALUATING PIPES

If you deem a pipe worthy of being included in your pipe collection, it matters little whether the pipe is new or whether it has been smoked. However, if its previous owners have smoked it to death, cracking either stem or bowl, it will be worth somewhat less since it will then have to be permanently relegated to the showcase.

As with all antique or art objects, the value of a pipe depends on its age, its condition, its maker or manufacturer, the quality of its workmanship, the scarcity of the particular type, and the current demand. Since few people would be expert on all these points about any particular pipe, it is easy to see why there are so few recognized pipe appraisers. The pipe's price is usually governed by the strength of the potential buyer's desire, and by how much he is willing to pay.

The collector may well find it difficult to determine how much an antique pipe is really worth. No catalog of collector's pipes and antique pipe values exists to inform him. Even attempting to quote a fair price for certain types of pipes is not easy, because no two pipes are exactly alike. They may be similar in many ways, yet the age, size, color, and overall condition of the individual specimen may greatly affect its value.

Old pipes retaining their original condition are the most valuable. If evidence turns up that some of the original parts, such as the stem or band, have been replaced, the pipe loses some value. This can easily be detected if the bowl shows signs of having been smoked but the stem displays no teeth marks. It's a good bet, in such cases, that the stem has been replaced.

The bowl of the pipe and its decoration largely set the price of the pipe. A plain, undecorated bowl naturally costs the least. Hand-work is also worth more than mass-produced work. A porcelain bowl decorated by a transfer or decal should cost less than a hand-painted one. An elaborately hand-carved meerschaum or briar, of course, always counts as a valuable item.

The best advice for a beginning collector is to patronize reputable pipe dealers. Their prices are likely to be fairly close to the real value of the pipe. This holds true for both modern pipes and older pipes. No one can deny a certain thrill one experiences in rummaging around antique shops in the hope of finding a bargain. But unless the hobbyist knows his subject well, he may very well pay an outrageous price for a common specimen.

If you spot a pipe which appeals to you, but you are not sure of its value, ask another collector to appraise it for you. If his appraisal agrees with yours, you can be sure of a reasonably good buy. However, if you see a bargain, grab it. Otherwise, your fellow pipe smoker may decide to make a nice addition to his own collection.

Chapter 10

Questions and Answers About Pipes

NO ONE BOOK can include within its covers all the facts about pipes and tobacco. An entire library would be required to deal with all the facets of pipe smoking. Although the contents of this book encompass a great deal of ground, they are by no means the last word on the subject. Both the new smoker and the veteran will often face baffling smoking problems and search in vain for their solution. In order to anticipate at least a few of these problems, some of the most frequently asked questions are presented here, together with the answers.

Q. *What is block meerschaum and how does it differ from any other type of meerschaum?*

A. A block meerschaum is a pipe carved from a single natural block of pure meerschaum. Meerschaum, mined in Eskersehr, Turkey, is a creamy white substance that has a distinctive flavor all its own. Only the most careful hand craftsmanship can produce this beautiful "heirloom" pipe.

Q. *Is it possible to salvage tobacco that has gone stale?*

A. "Stale" tobacco is more often than not simply tobacco that has lost its moisture. It can usually be salvaged simply by adding moisture to it. You might try spraying it with an atomizer.

Q. *When a good pipe goes sour, does it have to be discarded?*

A. Even the best of pipes may occasionally turn sour for some unexplained reason. To make a briar sweet-smoking again, first clean the pipe thoroughly as described in *Chapter 6.* Then plug the stem with a pipe cleaner, fill the bowl with a good pipe-cleaning fluid from your pipe dealer, and let the pipe stand overnight. Then remove the liquid cleaner, dry the pipe thoroughly and let it stand another twenty-four hours. Now break in the pipe again using mild tobacco.

Q. *Is there any way of replacing a broken pipe-stem?*

A. Most large pipe shops will perform pipe repairs. They may obtain an exact replacement stem from the factory that originally made the pipe, or they may use a new stem. In any event, the new stem will have to be carefully fitted to the original shank. The specal tools and skilled workmanship required to do this are available, but they may cost a few dollars. Unless the pipe is an unusually fine and treasured specimen, it may be cheaper to buy a new pipe. Meerschaum pipes are generally much more difficult to repair than briar pipes.

Q. *Is it possible to mix exactly the same blend of tobacco, time after time, so as to obtain an unvarying flavor and aroma for many years?*

A. It is possible to mix exactly the same blend time after time, but chances are the flavor and aroma will show subtle variations with every mix. There are many reasons for this. The same type of tobacco grown in different regions will have different tastes. Weather conditions will also affect the tobacco flavor from year to year. In order to produce an exact replica of a particular blend, the tobacco should be purchased from the same manufacturer and in the same cut. It should be carefully measured, mixed in exactly the same proportions, and at the same humidity. Also make sure that the age of the tobacco is approximately the same.

Q. *Do all pipes necessarily burn the tongue, or is it somehow possible to avoid tongue-bite?*

A. There are three main reasons why a pipe occasionally "bites" the tongue: (1) The pipe may not be clean. This is easily remedied by a thorough pipe-cleaning job; (2) You may be smoking too strong a tobacco. Ask your tobacconist for a slower-burning, milder blend; and (3) You may be smoking too rapidly. If so, learn to smoke slowly. Puff gently and pause between puffs.

Q. *How can a smoker know when a pipe is made from real briar? Do the words "Imported Briar" stamped on the pipe have any meaning?*

A. Unless one is an expert at distinguishing woods, no sure way exists of telling whether a pipe is real briar or not. The best guarantee is to obtain a pipe made by an established manufacturer and to buy it from a reputable dealer. The words "Imported Briar" do not insure quality in a pipe. Almost all briar, good and bad, is imported from countries bordering the Mediterranean. If you want to be certain of pipe quality, let a reputable dealer or pipe expert advise you.

Q. *Is any special equipment required to mix one's own tobacco blend?*

A. The only equipment needed to mix your own blend is a mixing bowl—a large salad bowl will do very well. A set of weights and a balance are useful, but not absolutely necessary. Unless you are very finicky about the fine points of blending, you will find that measuring by volume will give perfectly satisfactory results.

Q. *What pipe shape gives the coolest smoke?*

A. Pipes with long stems will definitely smoke somewhat cooler than sort-stemmed shapes. However, almost all pipes of normal length smoke about the same. Generally, the thicker the bowl walls, the cooler the smoke, since the thicker briar absorbs more heat. Canadian shapes have an oval shank that radiates heat more rapidly than the heavier shank.

Q. *How moist should tobacco be? Can excessive moisture harm the tobacco?*

A. A simple test can tell you whether your tobacco has the proper moisture content. Grasp a handful of tobacco and press it together for a few seconds, in your fist. Then open your hand. If the tobacco falls out in flakes from your open palm, is it too dry. If it stays pressed in a tight, hard ball, it is too moist. But if the tobacco remains as loosely packed ball, it contains an ideal amount of moisture. Overly moist tobacco is more susceptible to tobacco mold and will not burn easily. Dry such tobacco simply by spreading it out on a table in a war dry room for a few hours.

Q. *When a pipe with an uneven cake is completely reamed out, should it be broken in once more like a new pipe?*

A. Since the pipe has already been broken in, it is not necessary to go through the breaking-in process again. Therefore, it would be superfluous to use sweetening agents on the reamed pipe. All you need do is to build up the cake by smoking slowly clear to the bottom of the bowl.

Q. *What is the average life of a briar pipe? Does a pipe ever wear out?*

A. The life of a good briar pipe depends entirely upon its owner. With correct care and reasonably slow smoking, it should last the owner's lifetime. This applies especially to a quality pipe whose bowl is free from flaws or cracks which might start burn-outs. Properly cured quality briar is an extremely durable material; it will never "wear out" in the sense that an article of clothing or an automobile "wears out." So-called "worn-out" pipes are usually made of improperly cured woods, have been smoked to death day in, day out, have never been cleaned, and have been knocked about carelessly by their owners. A quality briar pipe, properly cared for, will outlast its smoker.

For free descriptive catalog of all Cornerstone
Library Publications write to:

CORNERSTONE LIBRARY, Inc.
Dept. 41
630 Fifth Ave.
New York 20, N. Y.